Christmas Quilts

by Marsha McCloskey

That Patchwork Place, Inc., Bothell, Washington

Title Page: **Princess Feather** by Sarah Lhamon, 1861, Mt. Vernon, Ohio, 88" x 88".
The Princess Feather was a very popular pattern after 1850. Many examples of the
design were made in the red and green fabrics then in fashion. The design can be traced
to the feather crest of the English Prince of Wales and has been worked in quilting and
crewel as well as in applique. This quilt is signed and dated in the center - a sure sign of
the maker's pride in her achievement. (Collection of That Patchwork Place)

ACKNOWLEDGMENTS

*Special thanks are extended to the many quiltmakers and collectors who
graciously loaned their quilts to be photographed:*

*Grace Bawtinheimer, Karey Bresenhan, Lillian Burch, Linda Carlson,
Suzanne DeBerry, Raenell Doyle, Bette Duncan, Maurene and George Ed-
wards, Donna Hanson Eines, The Ezra Meeker Historical Society, Trudie
Hughes, Donna Lake, Nancy Martin, Liz McCord, Judy Murrah, Lois Odell,
Carolann Palmer, Rosalie Pfiefer, Pam Reising, Alice Sanders, Freda Smith,
Judy Sogn, Fran Soika, Ann Stohl, Suzanne Wall, and Sharon Yenter.*

Although most of the quilts in CHRISTMAS QUILTS *have not been
published before, a few have appeared in other That Patchwork Place
publications, and five photograhs were supplied by Cyril Nelson from various*
QUILT ENGAGEMENT CALENDARS, *published by E.P. Dutton.*

Credits:
Photography . . . . *Carl Murray*
Zintgraff
Illustration and Graphics . . . . *Stephanie Benson*
Marsha McCloskey
Editor . . . . *Roberta Fuehrer*

That Patchwork Place ™

CHRISTMAS QUILTS ©

CONTENTS

INTRODUCTION

As a quilter, I have been to many quilt shows. One of the most memorable was an exhibit of red, green and white quilts at the Houston Quilt Market in 1982. Fine quilts from collections all over the country were gathered in this show entitled "Quilts: Christmas Memories." It was a visual feast with row after row of gorgeous red and green quilts.

My quilter's heart was stirred by the juxtaposition of the colors and the amazing artistry achieved by so many quilters using such a limited palette. One quilt in particular, a Feathered Star, captured my attention. I returned to it again and again to admire and to figure. My own version of the block used in that quilt is the Radiant Star on page 20.

I wanted to find a way to share the experience of that special exhibit with quilters everywhere and CHRISTMAS QUILTS is the result.

There are three parts to this book. The first is a mingling of Christmas lore and quilt history intended to set the stage for the gallery section and perhaps to give a new perspective on quilts at Christmastime.

The second section is the Christmas Quilt Gallery - a presentation in full color of a new collection of quilts in Christmas reds, greens and whites. This gathering includes both old and new pieces. Some are truly fine examples of specific designs. Others were chosen because they convey the joyous spirit of the season through color, imagery or style.

The third section of CHRISTMAS QUILTS is the pattern section. Most of the block patterns and applique motifs can be found in quilts in the gallery. All of the patterns look great in Christmas colors. Besides patterns, special help is given for choosing Christmas fabrics and for planning your own Christmas quilts. There is also a Glossary of Techniques in this section that gives tips and instructions for all phases of constructing a Christmas quilt.

CHRISTMAS QUILTS has been a happy project for me, and I hope you enjoy the book. May it help you, like Dickens' Scrooge, to keep Christmas in your heart all year long.

Merry Christmas!
Marsha McCloskey, 1985

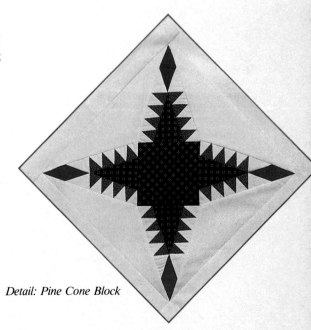

Detail: Pine Cone Block

CHRISTMAS QUILTS

Quilts are part of the homes and lives of quilt lovers year-round. Special quilts brought out only at Christmastime make the holiday brighter and help set the time apart from the rest of the year. Bonnie Leman, in Quilter's Newsletter Magazine, recalls such a special quilt from her childhood:

> Christmas dreams are happier under a Christmas quilt, I like to think. When I was a child my mother made me a quilt that I got to use only during the Christmas Season. Until the middle of December, it was stored on a special shelf with a sachet tucked inside. The ceremony of taking the quilt down from the shelf and putting it on my bed was an event I looked forward to with great anticipation.[1]

Another special Christmas quilt is mentioned in A PEOPLE AND THEIR QUILTS by John Rice Irwin. The quilt is not in the traditional Christmas colors of red and green, but is instead a typical Victorian crazy quilt with embroidered animals and much fine stitchery. The Lord's Prayer is embroidered in the center. Granny Irwin's son described her quilt in this way:

> I always thought it was the prettiest quilt I ever saw. But the only time she ever used it was around Christmas time. She'd get it out a few days before Christmas and use it as a bed cover til around the first of the year; then she'd put it away for another year. She made it, I think, about the time she was married in the late 1890s.[2]

1. Quilter's Newsletter Magazine (#157, November/December, 1983, p. 52.)
2. John Rice Irwin, A PEOPLE AND THEIR QUILTS, p. 42.

Special quilts at Christmas can only enhance the special feelings of the time. Who can imagine the children "nestled all snug in their beds" on Christmas Eve without quilts? Red and green quilts on the beds and walls lend pattern and texture to our surroundings and contribute an aura of special caring to the festivities.

Every year as Christmas approaches, national quilting publications and women's magazines offer patterns for holiday quilts and other projects. Christmas stories about beloved grandmothers, heirloom quilts, and "going home for Christmas" abound. Readers submit snapshots of their special quilts and wall hangings. The full-color photographs of calico ornaments and red and green quilts provide creative inspiration. Because quilters rarely discard patterns, collections for Christmas quilts grow every year.

Eventually, nearly every quilter will choose from the abundance of ideas and make a Christmas quilt or holiday wall hanging. These quilts, made as extra-special gifts or for decorating, have in common the colors and imagery of the Christmas season. In our culture, red, green and white are the traditional hues. Among the repeated images are stars, Christmas trees, bells, wreaths, holly and Santa Clause and all his trappings. Similar motifs are found on Christmas cards and package wrappings, in magazines and holiday decorations.

We have Christmas trees in our homes and evergreen wreaths on our doors. Special family gatherings are planned, gifts are given, and traditional foods are prepared. No other holiday merits half the preparation or level of joyous expectation. We need Christmas to make winter bearable. We need the break in routine that holiday festivities give us. The time set aside for friends and families, gift giving, singing and merrymaking is vital to our collective well-being. Imagine, if you will, a year without our winter festival of Christmas, and life would seem very drab indeed.

Quiltmakers or collectors can easily include their quilts in family holiday traditions. Even for those of us who never need an excuse to make another quilt, the idea of having special quilts to use and display at Christmastime is very appealing. Consider starting a bright, cheerful quilt in red and green during the holidays.

There is no need to put away the quilting frame just because it is Christmas; the creative clutter of quiltmaking is not out of place. A red and green quilt on the frame complements other holiday decorations and helps create a cozy atmosphere. Perhaps the quilt will take two or three Christmas seasons to finish if that is the only time it is worked on. When completed, it will be filled with the memories of the Christmastimes when it was being made, and rich in the spirit of Christmas whenever it is used.

Christmas Colors

To a quiltmaker, color is of paramount importance. In our culture we associate red, white and blue with the Fourth of July; pastel blue, pink and yellow with Easter; orange and black with Halloween; and red and green with Christmas. We are so accustomed to this color symbolism that red and green quilts are instantly identified as Christmas quilts, even if this was not the imagery and intention of the maker.

Red, green and white are the natural colors of winter in northern Europe where most of our Christmas traditions originated. White snow provides clear contrast with evergreens and red holly berries. To early peoples, the evergreen in winter symbolized never-ending life, and the eventual return of the fertile greens of spring and summer. In Christian liturgy, green stands for eternal life. There, too, red symbolizes the passion, the blood of Christ - also a sign of eternal life. The white of the snow signifies the purity of new beginnings.

On the color wheel, red and green are opposites. As complementary colors, they set up a visual resonance found in few other color combinations. The natural intensity of the colors coupled with cultural associations with Christmas make them the best choice for quilts at Christmastime.

Red and green quilts were the rage during the mid-1800s and many fine applique quilts survive from this period. One reason these colors were chosen for quilts that were expected to last for generations was because the dyes were considered reliable. In the 1830s the first solid-green dyes appeared. Green in fabric had previously been achieved by printing blue over yellow. Unfortunately, many of the solid-green dyes proved unstable and faded or changed color over time. Many fine quilts that survive appear as tan and red rather than the more vibrant green and red of the original dyes.

During this time when red and green quilts were popular, Christmas traditions as we know them in America were coming to full bloom. Christmas trees became fashionable, our image of Santa Claus with his white beard and fur-trimmed suit was crafted by cartoonist Thomas Nast, and the virtues of charity and brotherhood put forth in Charles Dickens' A CHRISTMAS CAROL captured the imagination of the nation.

That the red and green quilts of the period were intended as Christmas quilts is not certain, though many of the quilts seem to have holiday imagery. The popular Christmas plant, poinsettia, was introduced in this country in 1828 by the U.S. ambassador to Mexico, Joel Poinsett, and the vibrant red bracts appear in quilt imagery after that time. Christmas cactus, holly and pineapples (a traditional symbol of hospitality) and all kinds of applique flower and rose designs are present in the red and green quilts of the last century.

Images of Christmas

The shapes and patterns used in Christmas quilts are rich in tradition and symbolism. Many modern Christmas images have roots in Christian religious observances; others stem from the pagan customs of ancient cultures.

Christmas is a midwinter festival with roots that far predate the birth of Christ. The season falls during the darkest time of the year in the Northern Hemisphere. December 21 is the winter solstice, the shortest day of the year. As one travels northward, the darkness of night lengthens.

To ancient peoples, winter was a time of darkness, cold and evil spirits. Although people understood that darkness was normal in the cycle of seasons and knew that light and warmth would come again, ceremonies were held to ensure the return of spring and to restore fertility to the land. Just as the winter solstice marked the darkest time of the year, it also heralded the beginning of the return of the light, which was cause for much celebration.

The midwinter rites of light and fertility date long before Christianity. The contemporary observance of Christmas has developed over the centuries from borrowed and adopted elements of earlier midwinter celebrations. Many American Christmas traditions can be traced to the people of northern Europe.

Images we use in decorations and in Christmas quilts, such as stars, wreaths, holly and evergreen trees, are rich in ancient tradition and symbolism. We many times use the motifs with little thought to their meanings, but each Christmas image has a story and special significance.

Detail: In the Beginning-Christmas Quilt. Block by Dottie Smith

Holly

Dark, shiny green leaves and bright red winter berries symbolized life and rebirth to the peoples of northern Europe. Holly traditionally was brought inside to decorate at Christmastime and to ward off bad weather and evil spirits. It was considered unlucky to leave the holly up after New Year's Day or the Twelfth Night, and then it had to be burned, not thrown away. In quilting and applique, the versatile shapes of holly leaves and berries can be put to good use.

Wreaths

In quilts, there are wreaths aplenty. Favored as a quilting and applique motif for generations, quilters have given us many fine examples of wreath quilts. In the symbolism of Christmas, the circle of the wreath signifies eternity and everlasting life. Quilters regard it as a graceful and balanced motif in their art.

Detail: President's Wreath Block

Bells

In pagan midwinter festivals, the noise of ringing bells was supposed to drive off powerful evil spirits that thrived in a cold and lightless world. In the Christian world today, church bells ring, not to frighten away evil spirits, but to make a joyful sound of welcome for Christmas and to call people from their everyday occupations to celebrate. Salvation Army bells remind us of the charitable aspects of the season as we hurry about our Christmas shopping.

Bells in Christmas quilts can be worked as applique or quilting motifs.

Detail: In the Beginning -Christmas Quilt. Block by Grace Bartlett.

Candles

In Europe, it is customary to place a candle in the window on Christmas Eve to shed light and comfort in the darkness and perhaps to lead the traveling Mary to shelter. Special candles signal the progression of the Advent season and herald the birth of Christ, the incarnation of The Light into the world. In their solstice festival of Saturnalia, the pre-Christian Romans gave wax tapers as gifts. Early Christmas trees in America were lit with small candles - though, by many accounts, very briefly and always with a bucket of water nearby.

Detail: Christmas Candle Block

Stars

A star over Bethlehem led the wise men to the newborn Jesus. "...the star which they saw in the east, went before them, till it came and stood over where the child was. When they saw the star, they rejoiced with exceeding great joy." Matthew 2: 10-11. At Christmastime, the star of the Magi remains for us a powerful symbol; a magical guide in the darkness, a light in winter sky, a bringer of good news.

The Star of Bethlehem has long been a popular quilt pattern. Based on the Le Moyne Star, this many-diamond pattern sometimes extends to eight feet from tip to tip. The pattern for a small variation of the Bethlehem Star, the Blazing Star, is given on page 54 . Several examples of the Feathered Star, another intricate, old patchwork star design, are shown in the gallery.

BETHLEHEM STAR by Judy Sogn, 1984, Seattle, Washington, 34" x 34".

Christmas Trees

Christmas trees are a major part of our Christmas season and central to most holiday festivities. There is something magical about an evergreen tree in the house decorated with pretty things and shining lights.

Christmas trees became popular in the United States in the 1800s. The tradition was brought here by German settlers and the festive little trees were eagerly adopted. By the end of the century, the custom was widespread.

The German trees were small and generally displayed on tables. In America, larger and larger trees were used until they reached from floor to ceiling. Decorations of many kinds were used - candies, cookies, fruits, nuts, and flowers made of paper and cloth. Handmade and manufactured ornaments hung side by side with small candles which, though lovely, presented a real fire hazard.

Detail: Tree of Life Block

One predecessor of the Christmas tree in Germany was found in 16th century Miracle plays. The play traditionally presented on December 24 was about the fall of Adam and Eve and their expulsion from the Garden of Eden. The enactment was a way to educate the largely illiterate population, and illustrate to them the reason Christ had to be born into the world. Because Adam and Eve fell from grace and plunged the world into darkness, it was necessary that Jesus come to save it and bring it light. So the story of Adam and Eve was reenacted the day before Christ's birthday, Christmas.

The tree representing their temptation in the play was a small evergreen hung with apples. The people, impressed with the image, put up decorated trees in their homes on Christmas Eve. This was called the "Tree of Life" and often small figures of Adam and Eve and the serpent were placed beneath it. Eventually, other religious symbols were added to the decorations and the trees were known as CHRISTBAUM (Christ's Tree). Later, all kinds of fruits, nuts, cookies and candies decorated the trees to the point that some were called Sugar Trees.

In patchwork there are many traditional tree patterns. There are several versions of the Tree of Life, Tree Everlasting and Pine Tree. Ruth Finley places the inspiration for the appliqued Tree of Life designs with motifs commonly woven in the centers of oriental rugs in colonial times. The pieced Pine Tree design is said to have originated in New England. Whatever the design source, tree designs, especially in red and green, are often used in Christmas quilts because they resemble the decorated trees that grace our homes during the holiday season.

WOODLAND CHRISTMAS, by Carolann Palmer, 1985, Seattle, Washington, 17" x 24".

11

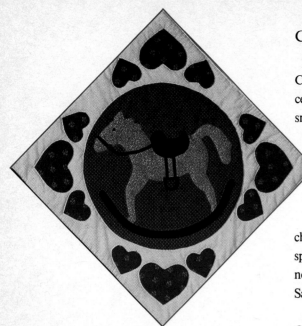

Detail: In the Beginning-Christmas Quilt. Block by Beth Black.

Childhood Memories

Christmas is a special time for children. In the story of the Nativity, the Christ Child was cherished and gifts were brought to honor him. The folk celebrations of Christmas in many countries include the giving of gifts and small festivities for children.

Santa Claus, in the tradition of St. Nicholas, is the special patron of children -- protecting them, overseeing their behavior and bringing them special gifts at Christmas. Many common Christmas symbols originated in nostalgic memories of childhood Christmases and imaginative concepts of Santa and his trappings.

The American perception of Santa Claus delivering gifts to children on Christmas Eve was crystallized by popular literature and news media of the 19th century. In his satirical KNICKERBOCKER'S HISTORY OF NEW YORK, Washington Irving described St. Nicholas as a figure flying through the air in a horse-drawn wagon to bring gifts to children.

Perhaps borrowing some aspects of Irving's descriptions, Clement Clark Moore later wrote a poem for his own children, "A Visit from St. Nicholas." Destined to become an American Christmas classic, the verse described Santa Claus as a "right jolly old elf," who traveled the sky in a miniature sleigh drawn by eight tiny reindeer.

Popular visions of Santa Claus in the early 1800s ranged from small elflike figures dressed in furs, who walked or drove wagons through the sky, to an imposing St. Nicholas clad in flowing bishop's robes, who rode a white horse. All were based on the jolly and venerable personifications of Christmas gift giving in Europe -- Kris Kringle, Father Christmas, Pere Noel and St. Nicholas.

The contemporary concept of Santa Claus probably can be credited to Thomas Nast, whose political cartoons appeared in Harper's Weekly during the 1860s. The large and jolly Santa Claus created by Thomas Nast had a full white beard and wore a fur-trimmed suit. Like all his predecessors, Nast's character brought Christmas gifts to children. Nast drew his Santa Claus making toys, riding in a magic sleigh and filling Christmas stockings. He was also pictured using a spyglass to see which children had been good and were to receive gifts and which children had been naughty and should be punished.

Many of these early images of Santa Claus became widely accepted and have endured through many generations to capture the imaginations of today's children.

Among the popular childhood visions associated with Christmas are Santa's sleigh and reindeer; toys, dolls and teddy bears; snowmen and ice skates; stockings; and candy canes and gingerbread men. The same images have been adapted to enhance Christmas quilts, especially those designed for children.

Children's quilts before the late 1800s were commonly small versions of larger quilt styles. Realism in quilt patterns for children can be traced to the late-Victorian concept of childhood as a special time in life. By the 1930s, children's quilts depicting Sunbonnet Sue, Overall Bill and stuffed animals were very popular. In the 1970s and '80s, quilters have extended realistic representations in quilts to anything that can be drawn.

Appliqued Christmas quilts are often made for children. Liz McCord's Christmas Sampler below skillfully re-creates nostalgic memories of a childhood Christmas.

CHRISTMAS QUILT, by Liz McCord, 1979, Redmond, Washington, 47" x 58". Stylized representations of childhood Christmas memories in machine applique make this quilt a real charmer.

CHRISTMAS CABIN AND WREATH, by Suzanne Wall, 1985, Seattle, Washington, 29" x 29".

Home at Christmas

Though there are always public holiday observations in church and the community, the most important Christmas celebrations are with family at home. Home shields us from the harshness of winter weather and family warms us with the food and gaiety of holiday festivities.

Two quilt patterns, in particular, remind us of home: the Log Cabin and House designs.

When it first appeared in the 1850s, the Log Cabin was worked most often with a red square in the center to signify the fireplace or hearth, the center of the home. The light and dark strips sewn around the center were called "logs," representing the log walls of early pioneer cabins. An example of a Log Cabin quilt in Christmas colors is shown on page 35.

Also embodying the special warmth of home are the House designs. With names like The Old Homestead, Little Red House and School House, these quilts were very popular during the late 1800s and have become a quilt design classic. Many were worked in red and white, making them doubly appropriate for use as Christmas quilts.

Detail: In the Beginning-Christmas Quilt. Block by Kathleen O'Brien.

14

CHRISTMAS CABIN IN THE COUNTRY, by Nancy Martin, 1985, Woodinville, Washington, 44'' x 44''. The School House block is a pictorial design that can be traced to the 1870s and has taken many variations. This nostalgic wall quilt combines houses, strip-pieced trees, and bright stars in red and green to complete the Christmas theme. Quilted by Gretchen Engle.

SCHOOLHOUSE, pieced by Nancy Martin, Woodinville, Washington, 1983, 62'' x 76''. Although called Schoolhouse, this design in red and white is reminiscent of home at Christmas, a very strong holiday theme. Quilted by Freda Smith.

Detail: Poinsettia Block

Christmas Flowers

Many of the red and green applique quilts of the 1800s depict roses and other flowers in wreaths and garlands. Although most flowers do not bloom in winter and are associated with other times of the year, the Legend of the Christmas Rose gives reason to believe some could be Christmas images. This lovely legend tells us that on the night the Christ Child was born, all the trees, shrubs and flowers bloomed in his honor. Also, the rose is commonly associated with the Virgin Mary, and in the 1800s, cloth and paper roses were often used to decorate Christmas trees. Another rose, known as the Holy Thorn of Glastony, by legend blooms every Christmas. It first grew when Joseph of Arimathea, fleeing from persecution after the resurrection of Jesus, came to England and on Christmas Day, plunged his staff into the ground at Glastony. The stick took root and blossomed, and supposedly has every year since.

The Christmas plant of Mexico, the poinsettia is seen in American quilt imagery after 1830. In the 1900s, when quilt design studios like Aunt Martha's and the Home Art Studio were the source for many quilt designs, pieced and applique poinsettia patterns were available. The Kansas City Star featured a Poinsettia pattern in 1931, and Stearns and Foster offered a pattern for a very realistic appliqued quilt, pictured on page 29.

DOUBLE NINEPATCH, origin unknown, 63" x 74". The Double Ninepatch quilt serves as a backdrop for a bed decorated with quilts in the Wreath and Pine Cone patterns and Log Cabin Christmas pillows. (Collection of That Patchwork Place)

CHRISTMAS QUILT GALLERY

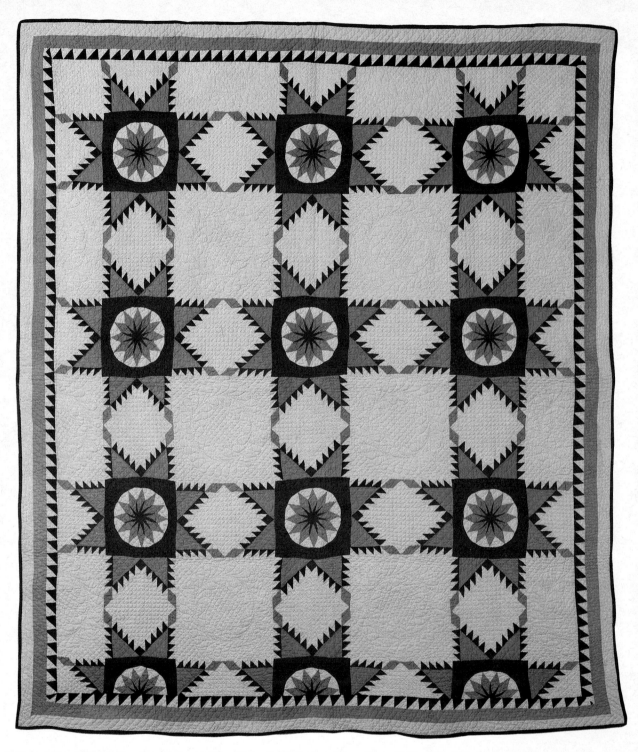

Feathered Star With Blazing Sun Center by Mrs. Rirhood, 1896, Grandview, Iowa, 70" x 80". This finely quilted piece is dated but not signed. It is in good condition, although what was once dark green has faded to a paler shade. The red, however, has retained its vibrancy. The traditional colors and star motifs place it firmly in the category of Christmas quilts. (Collection of Sharon Yenter, Seattle, Washington)

Right: **Feathered Star** by Nancy Martin Dearfield, c. 1847, Pleasants County, West Virginia, 81'' x 93''. Worked in red chintz and muslin, this quilt is typical of many Feathered Star quilts made in the 1800s. Perhaps the half stars were used to accommodate the size of the quilt to the batting, or to allow for a pillow tuck. (Collection of That Patchwork Place)

Below: **Pine Cone,** origin unknown, 70'' x 84''. This design is also known as a Feathered World Without End and as a Pineapple. The Pineapple is seen in many forms in old quilts as a symbol of goodwill and hospitality, fitting sentiments for the Christmas season. (Collection of That Patchwork Place)

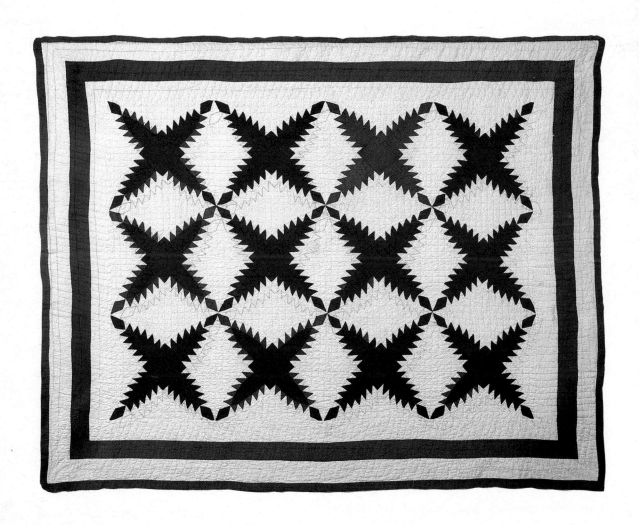

Above: Feathered Star Sampler quilt top by Marsha McCloskey, 1985, Seattle, Washington, 76" x 76". Many old Feathered Star quilts were worked in only two colors - commonly blue and white or red and white. This traditional sampler with its crisp red and white stars will be used as a Christmas quilt.

Left: **Radiant Star** by Marsha McCloskey, 1983, 20" x 20". This delicate Feathered Star variation suggests a snowflake.

Right: **California Star** by Donna Hanson Eines, 1984, Edmonds, Washington, 28" x 28". Finely quilted feather wreaths with red and green fabrics combine to make this an effective Christmas wall hanging.

Below: **Antique Star** by Mrs. Gilray, 1833, Scotland, 72" x 88". This exceptional red, green and white Feathered Star variation is a family quilt passed through several generations. The bright red accents are reminiscent of holly berries in winter. (Grace Bawtinheimer of Arlington, Washington)

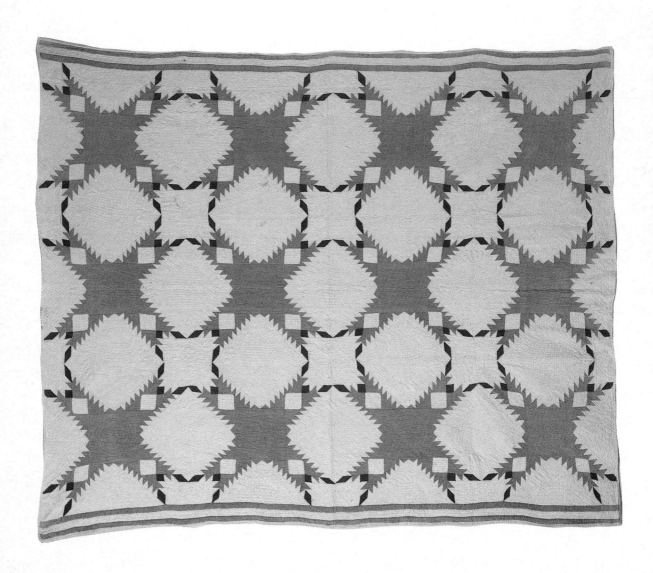

Double Peony, Edwards family quilt, c. 1825, Kentucky, 90" x 108". This glorious quilt recently emerged stained and discolored from a trunk where it has probably been for more than a century. Thirty-two Double Peony blocks are set alternately with thirty-one unpieced blocks which are embellished with stuffed work and trapunto. The Pineapple, a symbol of goodwill and hospitality, appears three times in the alternate blocks. The applique border of green and red perfectly frames this masterpiece. (George and Maurene Edwards, Seattle, Washington)

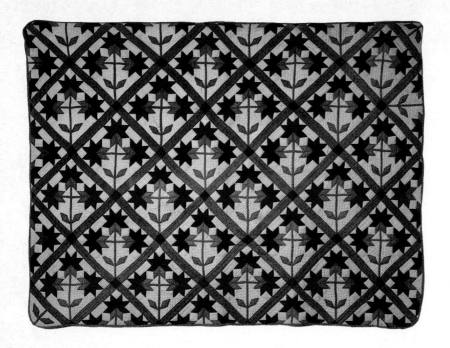

Left: **Bed of Peonies,** maker unknown, c. 1860, Kentucky, 67" x 90". Though the green has faded on this appliqued and pieced quilt, the vibrancy remains. The pieced Peony resembles a Poinsettia, the exotic plant from Mexico where it is known as the Flower of the Holy Night. (Collection of That Patchwork Place)

Below: **Peony** by Agnes Birnham, c. 1870-1890, Massachusetts, 100" x 100". Alternate blocks with fine quilting give this red and green Peony quilt an air of delicacy. Notice the corner variations in the Rose Vine border. (Collection of Sharon Yenter, Seattle Washington)

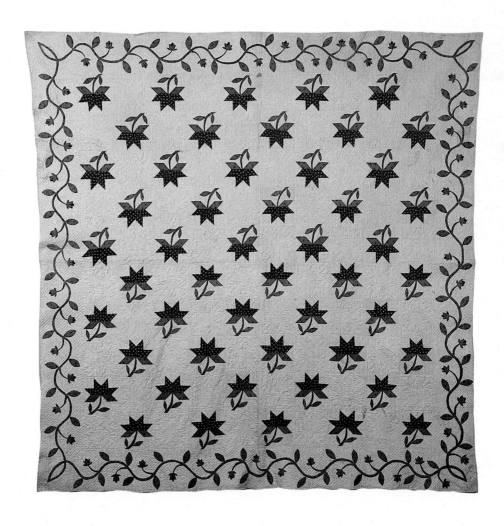

Zintgraff

Above: **President's Wreath,** maker unknown, c. 1930, Tyler, Texas, 74" x 82". The unusual setting of this popular wreath design creates a dynamic Christmas quilt in red and green. One may speculate whether the flower and leaf garland was intended for a border which was never added; or if it was used to add width to the quilt design. (Judy Murrah, Victoria, Texas)

Opposite Page, Top Left: **Flower Wreath Applique**, origin unknown, c. 1865, 68" x 86". The tan in this quilt appears to be the original color rather than transformation of an unstable green dye over time. Though a somewhat primitive applique, the dynamics of the overall design are exceptional. (Collection of Rosalie Pfieffer, Kent, Washington)

Top Right: **Cherry Wreath** by Linda Carlson and the Comforters, Tacoma, Washington, 1985, 86" x 86". Linda Carlson combined wreaths, bows, and swags in Christmas colors to create a holiday quilt which friends are helping to finish.

Bottom: **Rose Wreath** by Nancy Martin, 1985, Woodinville, Washington, 78" x 78". The wreath motif, a Christmas favorite, is combined with a meandering border in red and green to create a lively Christmas quilt. Quilted by Freda Smith. (Collection of That Patchwork Place)

Applique Holly Quilt, designed and made by Fran Soika, 1979, Novelty, Ohio, 104'' x 76''. All of the applique work in this quilt is done by the reverse-applique method, where the design is cut from the light-green background and then filled in with the dark-green elements. The holly berries are stuffed. Note also the exquisite contour quilting used throughout the piece. (Collection of the artist)

Left: **Rose Buds,** by Lynnie Gillespie LeSage, c. 1890-1900, Butte, Montan, 76" x 94". Lynnie LeSage, who was born in 1877, appliqued this quilt top as a young woman. It was quilted after she died at the age of 104. Note the realism of the appliqued rose leaves, which contribute to the overall delicacy of the design. (Collection of Ann Stohl, Yakima, Washington)

Below: **Tulips** quilt top, 78" x 78". The Tulip pattern and squares in this top are from the Laura Maxwell estate in Puyallup, Washington and were made around 1900. The quilt top was designed and set in 1984 by Mrs. Marilee Relf, the grandniece of local pioneer, Ezra Meeker. The wide red and green pieced border contrasts with the flowing applique Tulips to give this design uncommon strength. (Collection of the Ezra Meeker Historical Society, Puyallup, Washington)

Above: **Pomegranate,** origin unknown, c. 1930, 72" x 72". The pomegranate, here depicted in bold applique, was sometimes used in medieval Europe to decorate indoor trees during the Christmas season. (Collection of Sharon Yenter, Seattle, Washington)

Opposite Page Top: **Ohio Rose,** maker unknown, c. 1890, New York, 84" x 95". According to the Legend of the Christmas Rose, all the trees and flowers bloomed in celebration the night that Jesus was born. During the 1800s, paper and cloth roses were often used as decorations on Christmas trees. Size, excellent condition, and fine stipple quilting make this quilt a classic example of the rose design. (Collection of Sharon Yenter, Seattle, Washington)

Bottom Left: **Poinsettia,** origin unknown, 1930, 72" x 88". The scarlet Poinsettia, native to Mexico, was introduced in this country during the 1820s and has become a symbol of the Christmas season. This realistic applique pattern was added to the Stearns and Foster collection of quilt patterns in the 1930s. (Collection of Stearns and Foster)

Bottom Right: **Great Grandmother's Quilt** by Donna Lake, 1983, Noti, Oregon, 76" x 101". A Stearns and Foster pattern, this quilt was the third place winner in their 1983 Mountain Mist® Quilt Contest. The pattern catalog describes it: "The story of this quilt spans two continents. Originating in France, the design was that of a bridal quilt started in France and completed in this country". (Collection of Stearns and Foster)

29

Album, c. 1850, Baltimore, Maryland, 117'' x 117''. Judging from the red and green color scheme and the fact that holly is featured in the center of the top row, it would appear that this very handsome Baltimore Album quilt was intended as a Christmas gift. Photograph courtesy Thos. K. Woodard: American Antiques & Quilts. (Cora Ginsburg)

Above: **Christmas Tulips** by Bette
Duncan and the Busy Bee Quilters,
1984, Snohomish, Washington, 86" x
102". The red and green colors of this
quilt suggested the name to the many
quilters who helped produce it. Based on
a pattern from *McCalls How to Quilt
It!,* 1973, this quilt is very similar to the
Rose Buds quilt on page 27.

Right: **Oak Leaf Applique**, origin
unknown, c. 1860, 76" x 76". A variety of
red calico prints set on a white ground give
the illusion of winter snowflakes. (Collection of Ann Stohl, Yakima, Washington)

Mariner's Compass, with applique, 1855-1865, New England, 89 1/2" x 75 1/2". It is the slivers of white in the compass motifs that give real sparkle to this quilt, and the alternating red and green leaf forms give a delightful rhythm to the border. (America Hurrah Antiques, N.Y.C)

Above: **Mariner's Compass**, maker unknown, c. 1880, Ohio, 96'' x 96''. Although we think of St. Nicholas as bringing gifts to children, in legend, he was also the patron saint of sailors. Mariners depended on their compasses to guide them and on St. Nicholas to protect them on long voyages. Much of the charm of this red and white Mariner's Compass lies in the lavishness of the feather plume quilting. (Collection of Sharon Yenter, Seattle, Washington)

Left: **Georgetown Circle**, origin unknown, 74'' x 86''. The red and white design makes a perfect backdrop for Christmas decorations and festivities. (Collection of Ann Stohl, Yakima, Washington)

Above: **Delectable Mountains**, c. 1890, Berks County, Pennsylvania, 78'' x 80''. It seems apparent that the creator of this piece knew she was a magnificent quilter and set out to prove it here. (M. Finkel & Daughter)

Left: **Delectable Mountains** by Lois Odell, 1984, Kirkland, Washington, 54'' x 54''. This green and white wall quilt embodies the feelings of peace and plenty expressed in John Bunyan's description of the evergreen-covered new land in **Pilgrim's Progress.** The book was written in the 1600s, and the name Delectable Mountains was adopted early as a quilt pattern name in this country.

Above: **Schoolhouse**, 1930-40, New York State, 66" x 89". This fascinating geometric arrangement of the Schoolhouse pattern emphasizes the decorative importance of the white stripes, doors and windows of the red motifs. Strong red and green coloring makes a clear Christmas statement. (Kelter-Malce Antiques)

Right: **The Log Tree** by Carolann Palmer, 1985, Seattle, Washington, 67" x 88". Log Cabin blocks set diagonally create a forest of "trees". Bright red centers give a definite Christmas look.

Left: **Tree of Life**, maker unknown, 1883, Washington, 82" x 96". The asymmetrical set of this red and white tree quilt is an interesting solution to the problem of directional blocks. (Collection of Sharon Yenter, Seattle, Washington)

Below Left: **Christmas Pine Tree**, by Raenell Doyle and the Comforters, Tacoma, Washington, 1985, 71" x 71". Raenell Doyle designed the top and holly quilting motifs for the pieced blocks made by the Comforters. Adding red gives brightness and sparkle to the traditional two-color Pine Tree block.

Below: **Pine Tree**, by Comforts of Home, 1983, Ohio, 88" x 106". The Pine Tree motif is an old design used in colonial New England on coins and flags as a fitting symbol of freedom in a rich new land. The name of the block remains the same wherever it is found, having survived unchanged through the massive pioneer migrations that settled this country. (Alice Sanders, Cincinnati, Ohio)

Zintgraff

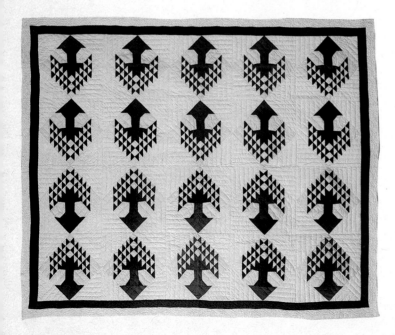

Above: **Tree of Life**, maker unknown, c. 1865-1875, Ohio, 74" x 82". Lively red and green triangles, straight set blocks, broad tree trunks, and the absence of borders combine to give this quilt a primitive but pleasing look. (Collection of Great Expectations)

Left: **Tree of Life**, origin unknown, 72" x 88". Evergreens have long been symbolic of good luck and renewed or everlasting life. Pine boughs and Christmas trees have been used as decoration at midwinter festivals for centuries. Several different green fabrics were used to piece the trees in this quilt. Some of the green dyes have faded more than others, creating interesting color variations. (Collection of Ann Stohl, Yakima, Washington)

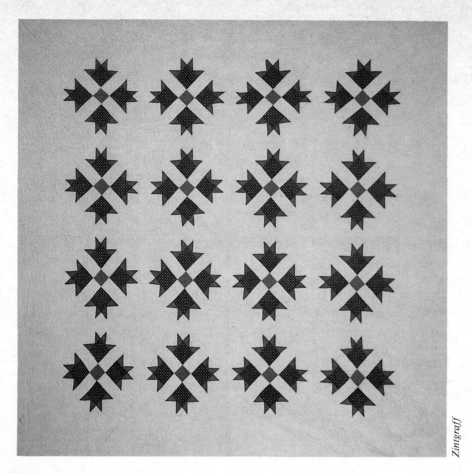

Zintgraff

Above: **Duck Paddle**, maker unknown, c. 1850, Pennsylvania, 94'' x 94''.   Also known as Goose Tracks, this old-fashioned design makes a cheerful Christmas quilt. Touches of yellow were often included with red and green in quilts made during the 1800s. (Collection of Apples of Gold)

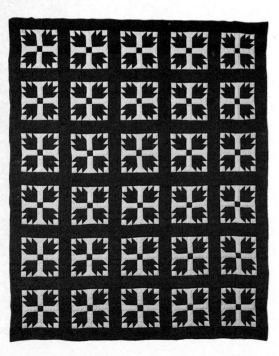

Below Left: **Bear's Paw**, by Lillian Burch, 1978, Kirkland, Washington, 87'' x 108''. Although most commonly known as Bear's Paw, this pattern has also been called Duck's Foot in the Mud, and Hand of Friendship. Strong red with white, this quilt would brighten any room at Christmas.

Below Right: **Double Irish Chain**, origin unknown, c. 1915, 99'' x 99''. This large red and green quilt was at one time cut in two and sewn back together across the middle; for what reason, we can only speculate. Strong use of red and green prints speak to us of Christmas. (Collection of Rosalie Pfieffer, Kent, Washington)

Above: **Goose In The Pond** by Marsha McCloskey, 1985, Seattle, Washington, 60'' x 60''. Ruby McKim called Goose in the Pond ''one of those homey old-fashioned names that grace so many patchworks''. Here, in red and green, this wall hanging will serve as a focal point for Christmas decorating.

Right: **London Squares,** origin unknown, c. 1945, 72'' x 88''. The red and white of this geometric design would add impact to Christmas decorating. (Collection of Rosalie Pfieffer, Kent, Washington)

In the Beginning Contest Quilt, 1984, Seattle, Washington, 78'' x 78''. The thirteen blocks were made by Kathleen O'Brien, Heki Henderson, Judy Rembsberg, Patty Heib, Joan Hanson, Dottie Smith, Tina Foley, Sidra Cowan, Rose Burkette, Beth Black, Jill Melton, Merilee Erickson and Grace Bartlett. The quilt top was designed and set by Marsha McCloskey and quilted by Marilyn Bacon.

Familiar images of Christmas have been combined in this exceptional sampler quilt. A Christmas tree, holly, wreaths, bells, a poinsettia, a star, a house, and a rocking horse reflect the rich symbolism of American Christmas culture in vibrant holiday colors.

The unique Christmas quilt unites the creativity of 13 winners in a Christmas block contest sponsored by In the Beginning-Quilts in Seattle. Chosen by customer vote from more than 80 entries, the winning blocks were set diagonally and framed by a sawtooth border. (Kathleen O'Brien, Seattle, Washington)

Planning

Color and Fabric Choice

Selecting red and green fabrics for a Christmas quilt takes time and patience, for not just any red will go with any green. Some leisurely experimenting is necessary to find a pleasing fabric combination. Choose some red and green fabrics and play with them — place them side-by-side, move and rearrange them, discard some and add others — until a satisfying selection develops.

Located directly across from each other on the color wheel, the reds and greens of Christmas are complementary colors. Red is a warm color that appears to come forward visually, while green is a cool color that recedes. Red agitates, green soothes.

In their pure forms, red and green are equal in value and intensity. Combining equal amounts of these colors can create almost a visual vibration, which can be calmed by using more of one color or the other or by adding a white background.

Most fabric colors are not pure colors. Instead, they are shades (dark colors), tones (grayed colors), and hues that seem to have a large amount of blue or yellow in them. Colors, especially prints, vary in intensity. For best results, select the main red and green fabrics in a similar color intensity. For example, combine a dark green with a dark red.

It is also important to consider the temperature of colors. Red, normally a warm color, can have a blue cast that makes it cool; green, normally a cool color, can have a yellow cast that makes it warm. For the most harmonious effect, it is usually best to use cool reds with cool greens, etc. The temperature of the background fabric must be considered as well. Muslin or ecru, for instance, is a much warmer and softer choice than pure white.

When choosing prints, pay attention to their visual texture. Visual texture is the way a print looks. Is it spotty, smooth, dappled, linear, rhythmic or swirly? Are the figures in the print far apart or close together, large or small? Mix large prints with small prints; mix flowery allover designs with tiny dots or checks. Too many similar prints can create a dull, uninteresting quilt surface.

The amount of white in a print can affect its intensity. To avoid mistaking prints with white in them for other values, look at them from across the room. A white figure on a red background, for instance, can appear red close up but look quite pink from a distance.

Study the gallery section of this book. The quilts fall into two general categories — background quilts and focal point quilts. Large two-color quilts with a large amount of white make lovely backdrops for Christmas festivities and other holiday decorations. Darker, smaller pieces made in three colors are visually more active and command more attention, becoming focal points.

Consider also, that some patterns will attract more attention than others. A simple geometric design with no identifiable cultural symbolism will draw less attention than a well-known image, such as a star, house or tree. Take time to decide the way a Christmas quilt is to function in your decorating scheme during the holidays and plan accordingly.

For best results, select lightweight, closely woven 100% cotton fabrics. Polyester content may make small patchwork pieces difficult to cut and sew accurately. Preshrink all fabrics before use. Wash light and dark colors separately with regular laundry detergent and warm water. If you suspect that a dark color might run, rinse it separately in plain warm water until the water remains clear. Dry fabrics in the dryer and press them well before cutting.

Unit Blocks

There are 20 patchwork Christmas designs in the pattern section. Stars and trees, flowers, wreaths and holly, and lively geometrics are presented for making applique and pieced Christmas quilts. All look smashing worked in red, green and white. Most of the unit block designs are from quilts in the gallery section.

The Christmas blocks can be used for quilts or incorporated in other patchwork projects for the holidays. Consider making pillows, table runners, tree skirts, aprons and wall quilts, as well as full-sized quilts.

Quilt Sets

When unit blocks are sewn together in a quilt top, the total design is called the "set". There are literally thousands of unit block designs and relatively few basic ways to put them together. Yet, an amazing number of quilt top designs are possible. You will need to decide the best way to set your Christmas blocks. The basic methods are outlined below.

Blocks can be set straight-on or on the diagonal. Some look best sewn together side-by-side, like the Pine Cone blocks in the quilt on page 19. The secondary design at the corners where the blocks meet would be lost in any other set.

Other blocks look best separated by alternate blocks or lattice strips. These are called "set pieces" and can be plain or pieced. Take time to play with completed blocks and arrange them in different ways. Lay the blocks out on the floor or bed. Vary spatial arrangements. Try diagonal and straight-on sets and think about appropriate border treatments.

Plain or pieced lattices can be used to separate unit blocks.

The coloring of the set pieces is a very important part of the quilt's total look. Set pieces that are the same color as the background of the unit blocks float the design motifs, while those cut from contrasting fabric outline each block and emphasize its squareness.

Feel free to experiment with different sets. Although I usually have a quilt plan in mind when I make a group of unit blocks, I like to play a bit to see how the blocks look in different arrangements when they are finished. Blocks often appear quite different made up than they looked drawn on paper, and original quilt plans may need adjustments.

Borders

Borders are a very important part of a good quilt plan and function to frame a quilt design. They visually contain it and keep it from running off the edge. Borders emphasize and enhance the central quilt design if they relate to it properly in scale, motif and color. Borders can be simple or complex. Pieced or appliqued designs can be effectively incorporated to frame a central motif.

If you choose plain borders with straight sewn corners, first sew borders to the long sides of the quilt, then to the width. Striped fabrics make lovely quilt borders, but the corners must be mitered to make the design turn the corner gracefully. Mitering corners is not difficult and worth the effort in many design situations. It is especially important to miter corners when using stripes or multiple plain borders.

Make a small Christmas wall quilt with one Tree of Life block embellished with Sprig of Holly. Shown here are multiple borders with mitered corners.

Quilt Size

The size of your quilt will depend on its intended function. You will need to make a quilt plan before you can buy fabric and begin sewing. A quilt plan can be a scale drawing of a quilt design, on 1/8'' graph paper. From such a plan, it is easy to tell the number of unit blocks and set pieces that will be needed to complete a given quilt, as well as finished dimensions of plain borders and the number of repeats in patchwork borders.

The drawing on page 44 is an example of a quilt plan. To make the Double Ninepatch quilt larger or smaller, add or subtract blocks, set pieces and borders until the desired size is reached.

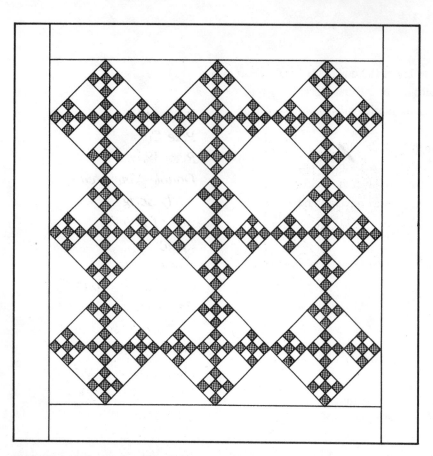

This very simple Double Ninepatch becomes an effective allover quilt design when the blocks are set with unpieced alternate blocks in the background color of the unit blocks. Here plain, background color borders are shown with straight sewn corners.

Figuring Yardage

Base yardage requirements on a good quilt plan and follow these steps.

1. Identify and make templates for all the shapes in the quilt design, i.e., pieces in the pattern blocks and the set pieces (lattices or alternate blocks). You don't have to make templates for large border pieces; knowing their dimensions is enough.

2. For each template, write the number of pieces to be cut from each fabric in your design.

3. Armed with shapes, sizes and numbers, proceed to figure out how many of each template will fit on the usable width of the fabric. With fabric that is 45'' on the bolt, you can really count on a usable width of only 42''. Selvages should be cut off and you must allow for some shrinkage. For example, twelve 8 1/2'' squares are needed as set pieces in the quilt plan. Divide 42'' by 8.5'' and find that four complete squares can be cut from the width of the fabric. Each set of four squares requires 8.5 linear inches of fabric. To get 12 squares, 3 x 8.5'' or 25.5 linear inches of fabric are needed. This is nearly 3/4 yard (27''), but to buy only 3/4 yard would be cutting it pretty close. Go on to the next highest eighth of a yard and buy 7/8 yard. It is a good idea to buy at least four extra inches of a fabric to allow for shrinkage, straightening and cutting mistakes. Complete this process for each shape and fabric in the quilt plan. Total the amounts and you are ready to buy.

CHRISTMAS PATTERNS

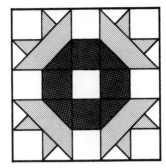

Radiant Star
Pine Cone
Rose Wreath
Double Ninepatch
Holly Sprig
Bed of Peonies
Peony
Blazing Star
Goose in the Pond
Bear's Paw
Mexican Rose
Duck Paddle
Hands All Around
Georgetown Circle
Pine Tree
Tree of Life
School House
Christmas Candle
Delectable Mountains
Swag Border

Templates

To make each unit block, you will need a set of pattern pieces or templates. Carefully trace the templates from the book onto graph paper or tracing paper. Trace accurately and transfer to the paper all information printed on the templates in the book.

Each template for the unit blocks is labeled with a number, the design name, the finished block size, and the number to cut for one block. A notation such as "Cut 4 + 4" indicates the same template is used for two colors in the design. An "R" in a cutting notation means "reverse". The pieces are mirror images: cut the first number of pieces with the template face up and then flip it over face down to cut the remainder. Where it is needed, shapes are marked with a grain line. All templates, except those for applique, include 1/4" seam allowance.

Roughly cut out the pattern pieces (outside the cutting line). Glue each one to a thin piece of plastic (x-ray film is good) or lightweight posterboard. Cut out the paper pattern and its stiffening together. Be precise. Make a template for each shape in the design.

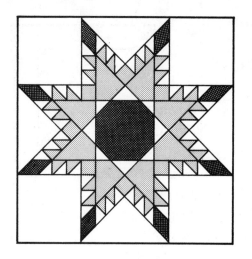

RADIANT STAR
15" block

This Feathered Star variation makes a great wall quilt all by itself — or repeated in a larger piece. Use Bias-Strip Piecing for the "feathers" and greatly reduce your cutting and sewing time.

Piecing Sequence
Unit A: Center, Make 1

Unit B: Make 4

Sew   Sew

NOTE: If bias-strip piecing is used for the half-square triangles of the "feathers", use template #4 to make 32 bias cut units and cut only 16 of template #5.

Unit C: Make 4

Sew the remaining portions of these seams last.

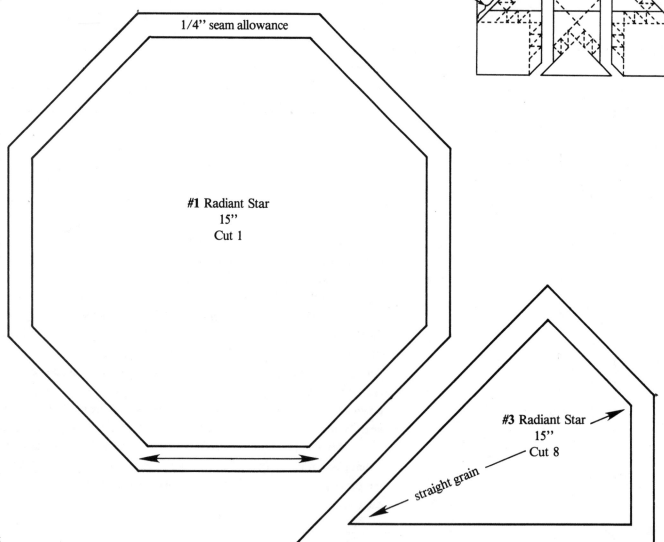

1/4" seam allowance

#1 Radiant Star
15"
Cut 1

#3 Radiant Star
15"
Cut 8

straight grain

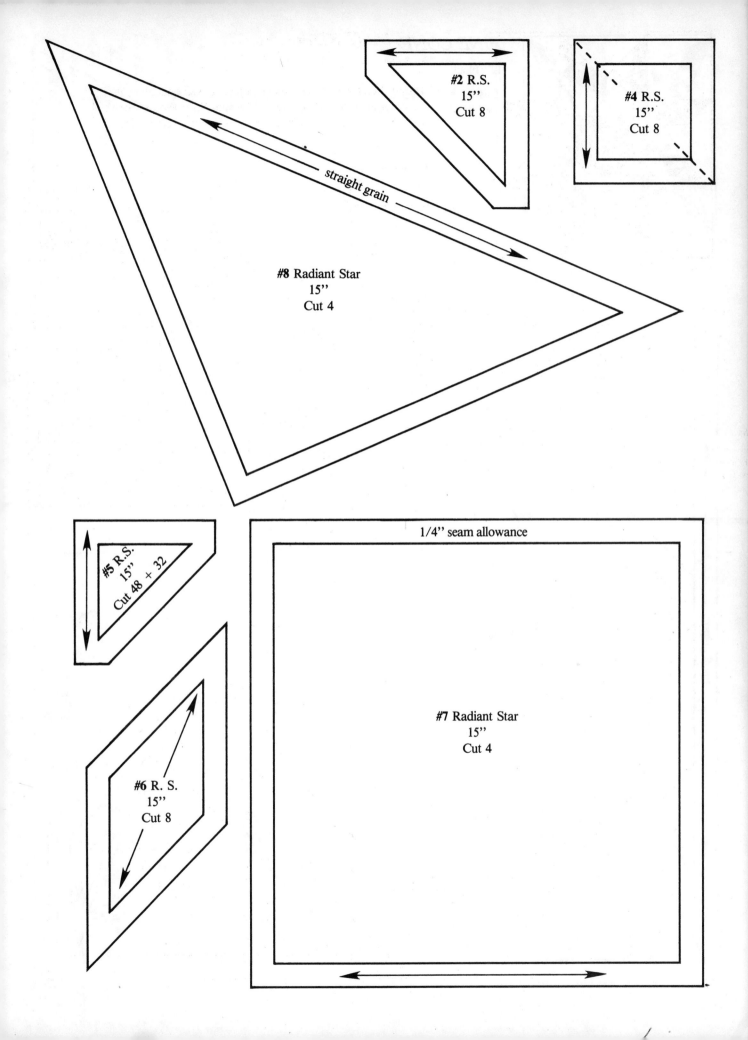

#2 R.S.
15''
Cut 8

#4 R.S.
15''
Cut 8

straight grain

#8 Radiant Star
15''
Cut 4

#5 R.S.
15''
Cut 48 + 32

1/4'' seam allowance

#7 Radiant Star
15''
Cut 4

#6 R. S.
15''
Cut 8

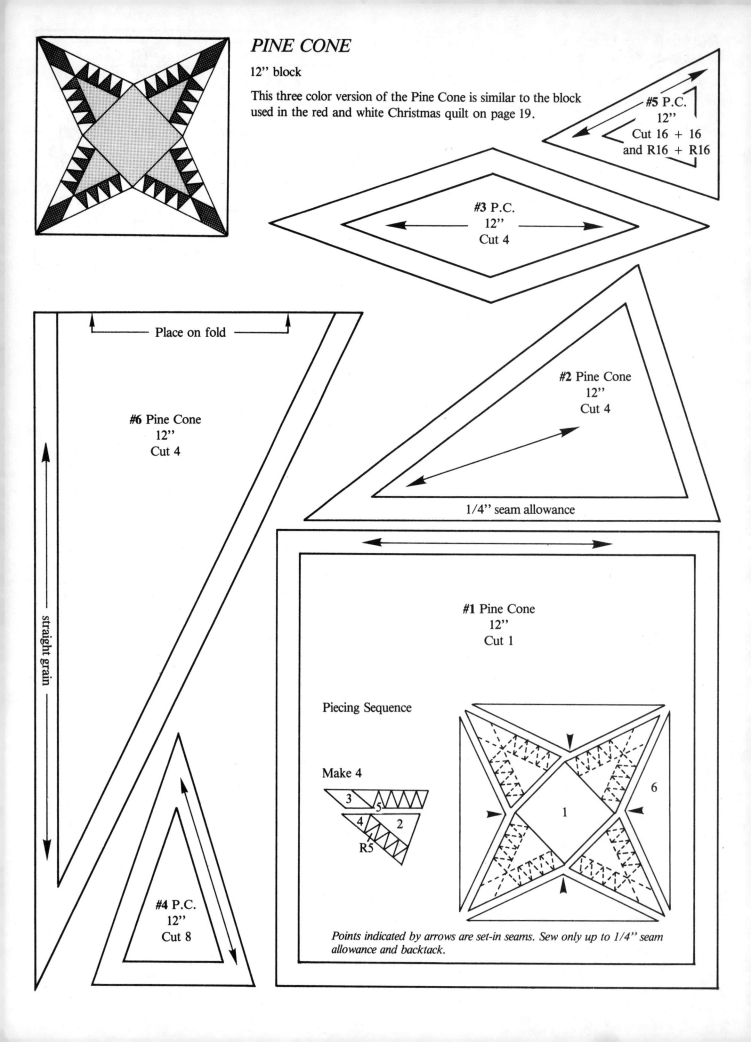

PINE CONE

12" block

This three color version of the Pine Cone is similar to the block used in the red and white Christmas quilt on page 19.

#5 P.C.
12"
Cut 16 + 16
and R16 + R16

#3 P.C.
12"
Cut 4

#2 Pine Cone
12"
Cut 4

1/4" seam allowance

Place on fold

#6 Pine Cone
12"
Cut 4

straight grain

#1 Pine Cone
12"
Cut 1

Piecing Sequence

Make 4

#4 P.C.
12"
Cut 8

Points indicated by arrows are set-in seams. Sew only up to 1/4" seam allowance and backtack.

ROSE WREATH

14" block

This lovely Rose Wreath is similar to the one in Nancy Martin's quilt on page 25. Cut a 15" square of background fabric, (trim to size after applique is finished), fold it in half both ways and press the folds. Position the flowers on these creases. To help position the stems, use a compass set at 4.5" to draw a very light pencil circle on the fabric square. See page 68 for further instructions for Paper-Patch Applique.

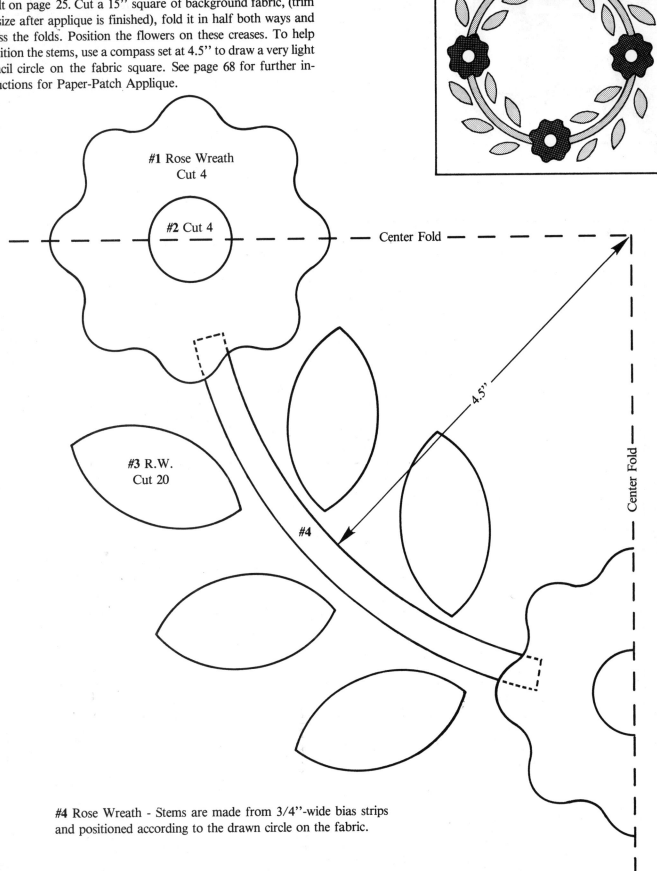

#1 Rose Wreath
Cut 4

#2 Cut 4

Center Fold

4.5"

#3 R.W.
Cut 20

#4

Center Fold

#4 Rose Wreath - Stems are made from 3/4"-wide bias strips and positioned according to the drawn circle on the fabric.

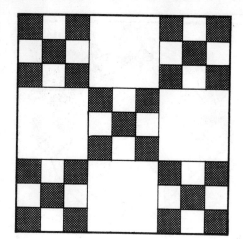

DOUBLE NINEPATCH

9" block

Shown in crisp red and white on page 16, this simple design is great as a background quilt for Christmas decorations and festivities. It could be pieced easily and quickly using the Straight-grain Strip Piecing technique described on page 66. Set the blocks alternately with unpieced squares (cut 9 1/2" to include seams) to complete the overall design. See page 44 for a Double Ninepatch quilt plan.

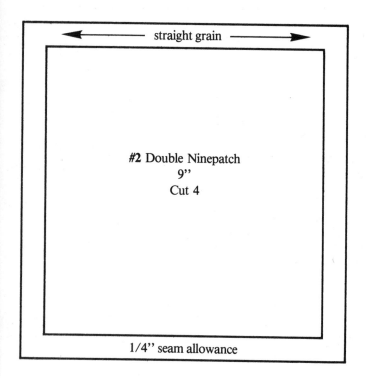

straight grain

#2 Double Ninepatch
9"
Cut 4

1/4" seam allowance

Piecing Sequence

Make 5

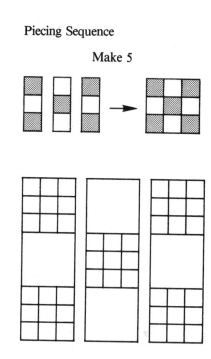

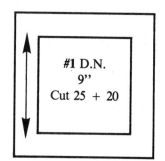

#1 D.N.
9"
Cut 25 + 20

HOLLY SPRIG

Add a bit of good luck to a Christmas quilt with this Holly Sprig designed as a quilting motif by Raenell Doyle for her Christmas Pine Tree quilt shown on page 36. This versatile little motif can be used for quilting or applique designs. See Paper-Patch Applique on page 68. When marking a Holly Sprig for quilting, make a stiffened template of the leaf to trace around and use a penny for the berries.

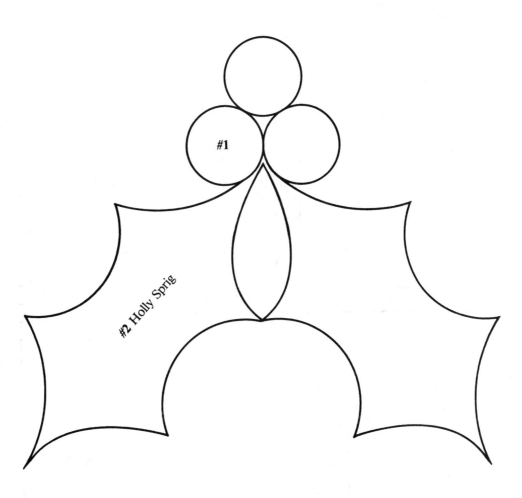

#1

#2 Holly Sprig

BED OF PEONIES

14" block
This pieced and appliqued Bed of Peonies is similar to the block in the Christmas quilt pictured on page 23.

Piecing Sequence

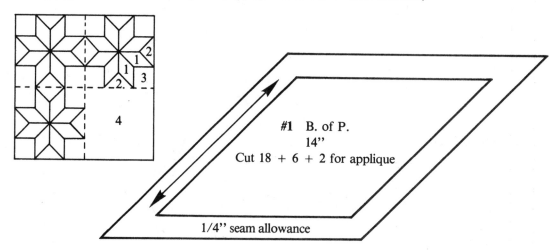

1.   Make 6   Make 3   Make 3

      A   B   C

Points indicated by arrows are set-in seams. Sew only up to 1/4" seam allowance and backtack.

2.   Flower units   3.   Set the three flower units together with piece #4.
      Make 3   4.   Applique stem and leaves in place. (Applique stem is 3/4"-wide finished.)

#1   B. of P.
     14"
     Cut 18 + 6 + 2 for applique

1/4" seam allowance

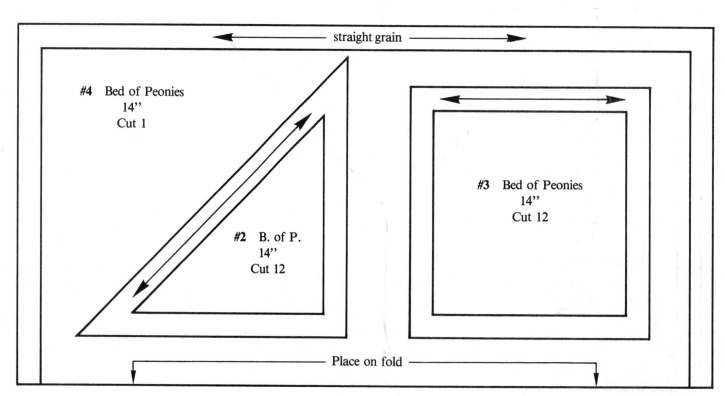

straight grain

#4   Bed of Peonies
     14"
     Cut 1

#2   B. of P.
     14"
     Cut 12

#3   Bed of Peonies
     14"
     Cut 12

Place on fold

PEONY

8" block

A version of this pieced and appliqued block is shown set with alternate unpieced blocks on page 23. Piece the block according to the Piecing Sequence below and applique the stem and leaves last.

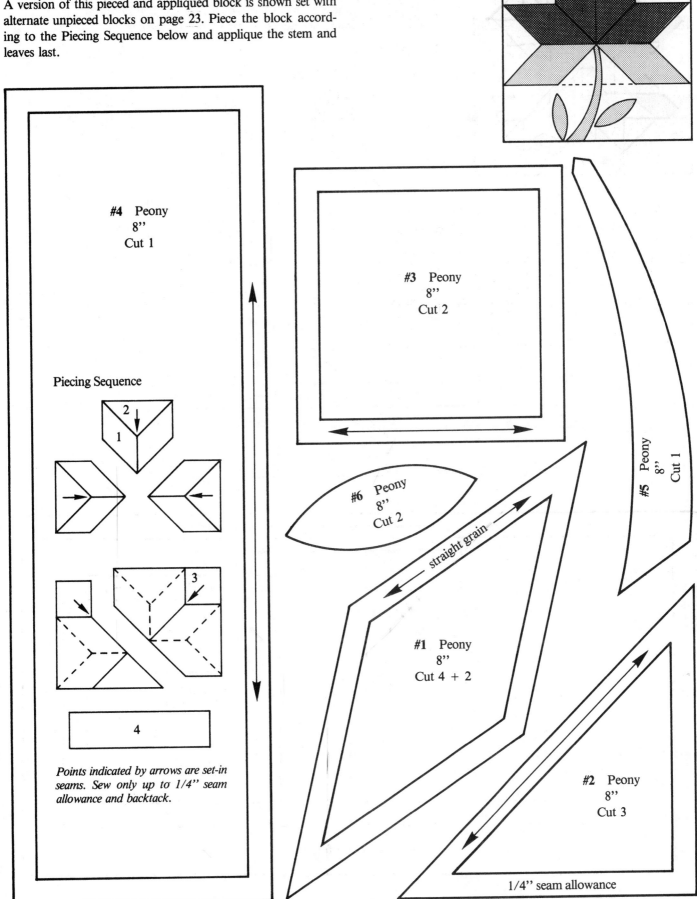

#4   Peony
8"
Cut 1

Piecing Sequence

Points indicated by arrows are set-in seams. Sew only up to 1/4" seam allowance and backtack.

#3   Peony
8"
Cut 2

#6   Peony
8"
Cut 2

#5   Peony
8"
Cut 1

straight grain

#1   Peony
8"
Cut 4 + 2

#2   Peony
8"
Cut 3

1/4" seam allowance

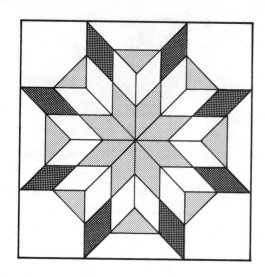

BLAZING STAR

12" block

The Blazing Star is a small version of the Star of Bethlehem, a favorite old patchwork design with a Christmas theme.

Piecing Sequence

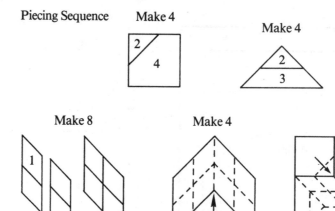

Make 4

Make 4

Make 8

Make 4

Points indicated by arrows are set-in seams. Sew only up to 1/4" seam allowance and backtack.

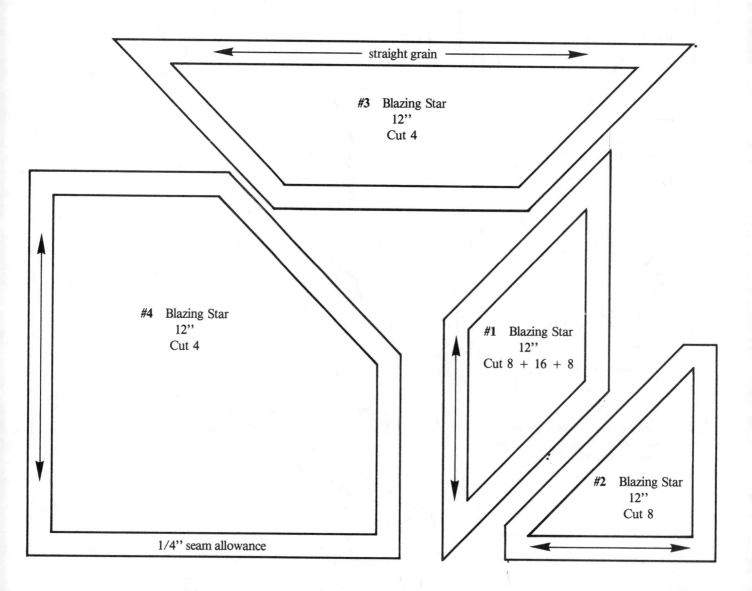

straight grain

#3 Blazing Star
12"
Cut 4

#4 Blazing Star
12"
Cut 4

#1 Blazing Star
12"
Cut 8 + 16 + 8

#2 Blazing Star
12"
Cut 8

1/4" seam allowance

GOOSE IN THE POND

12" block

The Goose in the Pond Christmas quilt is shown on page 39. Although templates for each piece are given here, this block could easily be adapted to strip piecing techniques.

Piecing Sequence

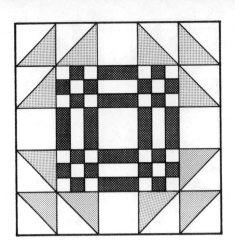

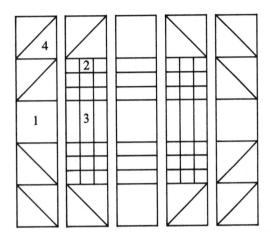

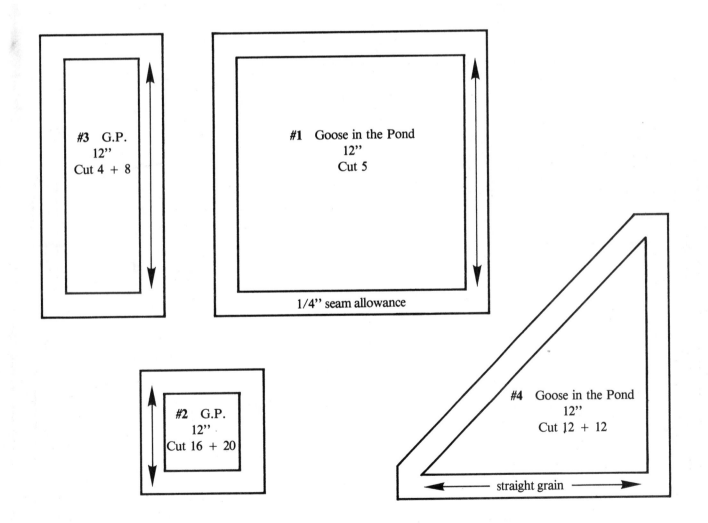

#3   G.P.
12"
Cut 4 + 8

#1   Goose in the Pond
12"
Cut 5

1/4" seam allowance

#2   G.P.
12"
Cut 16 + 20

#4   Goose in the Pond
12"
Cut 12 + 12

straight grain

BEAR'S PAW

10" block

The Bear's Paw is shown in red and white on page 38. Try the bias strip piecing technique (p 67) for the half triangle squares in this design.

Piecing Sequence

Make 4

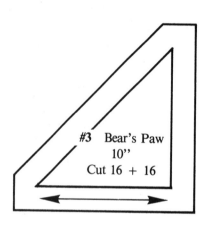

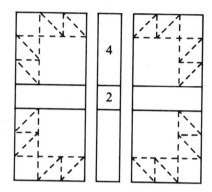

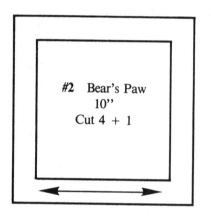

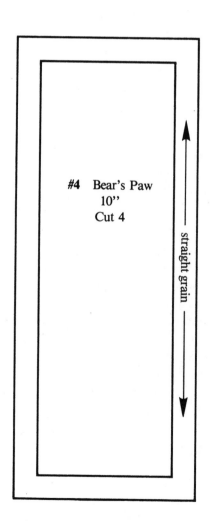

#2 Bear's Paw
10"
Cut 4 + 1

#3 Bear's Paw
10"
Cut 16 + 16

1/4" seam allowance

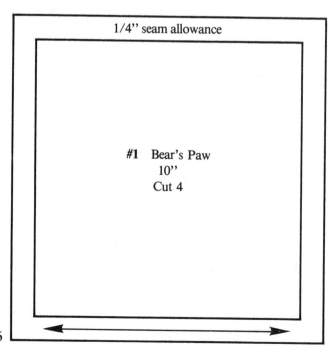

#1 Bear's Paw
10"
Cut 4

#4 Bear's Paw
10"
Cut 4

straight grain

25-PATCH DESIGNS

These four 10" pieced blocks are similar 25-patch designs and share the same templates. A red and white Georgetown Circle quilt is shown on page 33. All of these blocks look super in red, green and white.

The Mexican Rose and Duck Paddle blocks share the same templates and piecing sequence. It is a color change of piece #6 that makes the blocks different.

MEXICAN ROSE

10" block

DUCK PADDLE

10" block

Template **#1**, cut 1 + 4; **#2**, cut 4; **#4**, cut 4; **#5**, cut 8 + 8; **#6**, cut 4.

Piecing Sequence Make 4 Make 4

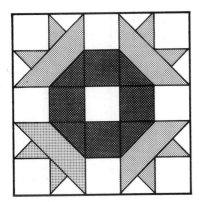

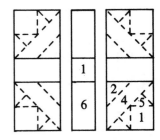

HANDS ALL AROUND

10" block

Template **#1**, cut 4 + 9; **#2**, cut 4; **#4**, cut 4; **#5**, cut 8 + 8.

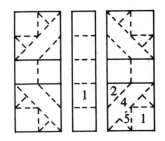

Piecing Sequence

GEORGETOWN CIRCLE

10" block

This is another block that could quickly be pieced using strip piecing techniques.

Template **#1**, cut 4 + 5; **#2**, cut 16 + 16.

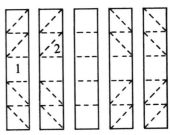

Piecing Sequence

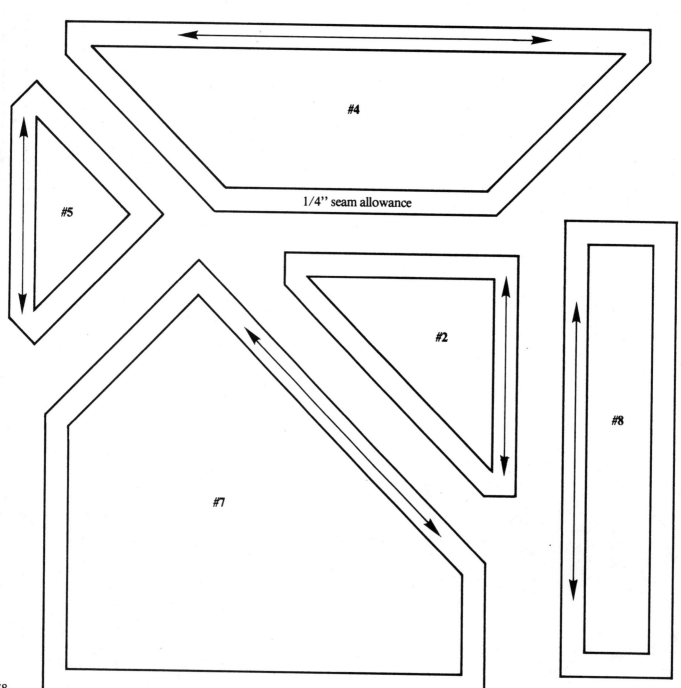

TEMPLATES

Use these templates for the Mexican Rose, Duck Paddle, Georgetown Circle, Hands All Around, Pine Tree and the Tree of Life.

#6

straight grain

#1

#4

#5

1/4'' seam allowance

#2

#8

#7

#3

PINE TREE AND TREE OF LIFE

There are many patchwork tree design variations. The 10" Pine Tree and 12" Tree of Life were designed to use the same templates as the 25-patch variations on the previous pages. They are presented here as basic tree designs. You may want to make the trunks thicker to look more like the tree designs in the Christmas quilts on pages 36 and 37. The tree designs are an excellent place to use Bias-Strip Piecing to make the many half-square triangles.

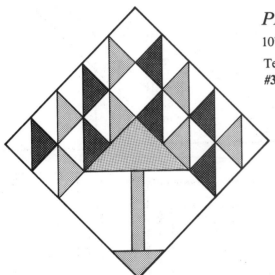

PINE TREE

10" block

Template **#1**, cut 1; **#2**, cut 8 + 7 + 14; **#3**, cut 1; **#7**, cut 1 R 1; **#8**, cut 1.

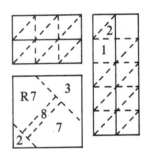

Piecing Sequence

TREE OF LIFE

12" block

Template **#1**, cut 1 + 2; **#2**, cut 6 + 10 + 23; **#3**, cut 1 + 2; **#7**, cut 1 R 1; **#8**, cut 1.

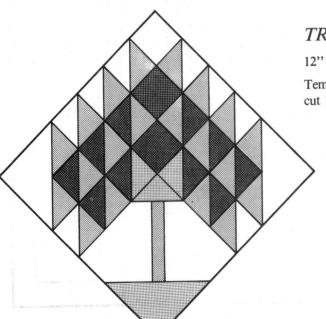

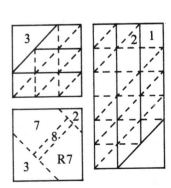

Piecing Sequence

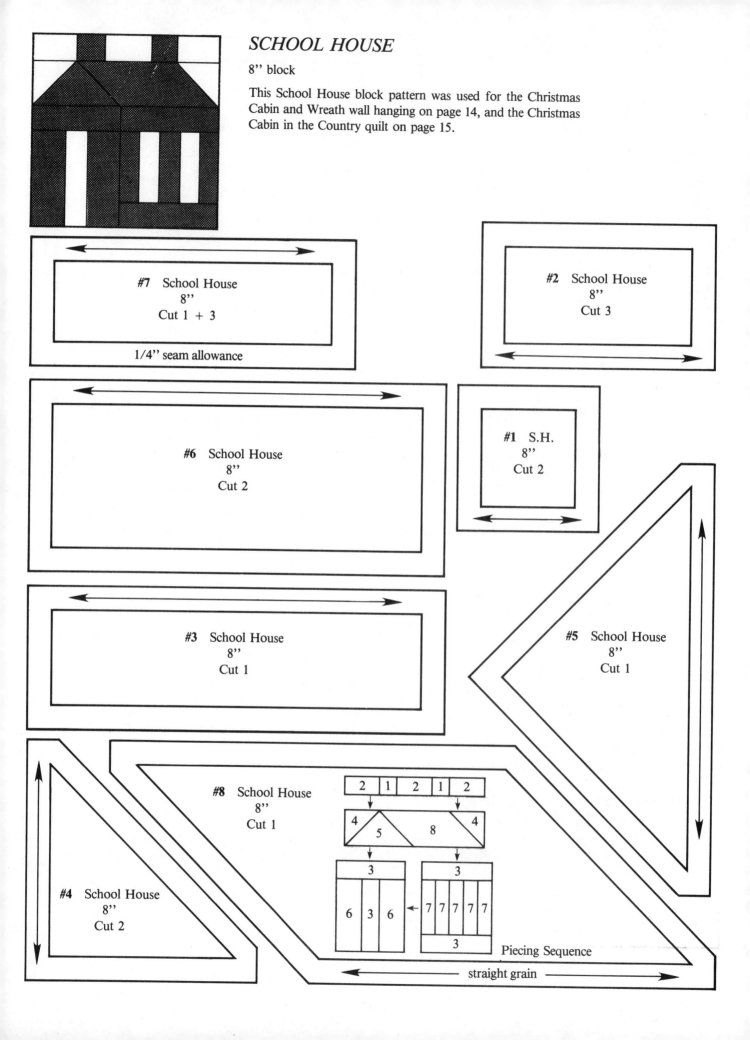

SCHOOL HOUSE

8" block

This School House block pattern was used for the Christmas Cabin and Wreath wall hanging on page 14, and the Christmas Cabin in the Country quilt on page 15.

#7 School House
8"
Cut 1 + 3

1/4" seam allowance

#2 School House
8"
Cut 3

#6 School House
8"
Cut 2

#1 S.H.
8"
Cut 2

#3 School House
8"
Cut 1

#5 School House
8"
Cut 1

#8 School House
8"
Cut 1

| 2 | 1 | 2 | 1 | 2 |

| 4 | 5 | 8 | 4 |

| 3 | | 3 |

| 6 | 3 | 6 | | 7 | 7 | 7 | 7 | 7 |

| | | | 3 |

Piecing Sequence

#4 School House
8"
Cut 2

straight grain

CHRISTMAS CANDLE

8" x 5" block

The Christmas Candle, pictured on page 10, is an enduring Christmas symbol.

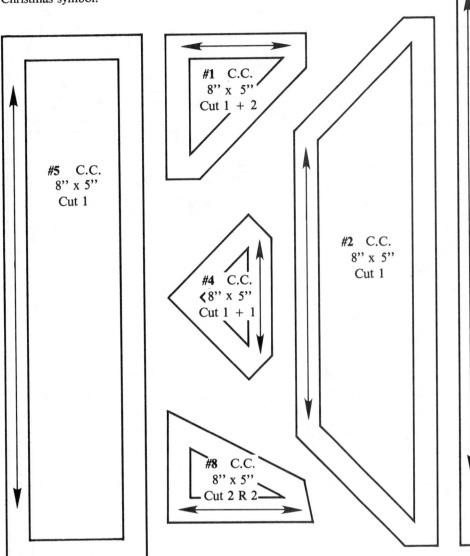

#1 C.C.
8" x 5"
Cut 1 + 2

#5 C.C.
8" x 5"
Cut 1

#2 C.C.
8" x 5"
Cut 1

#4 C.C.
8" x 5"
Cut 1 + 1

#8 C.C.
8" x 5"
Cut 2 R 2

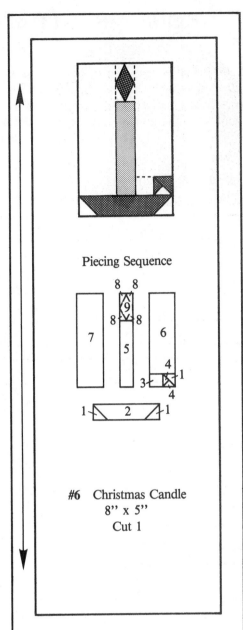

Piecing Sequence

#6 Christmas Candle
8" x 5"
Cut 1

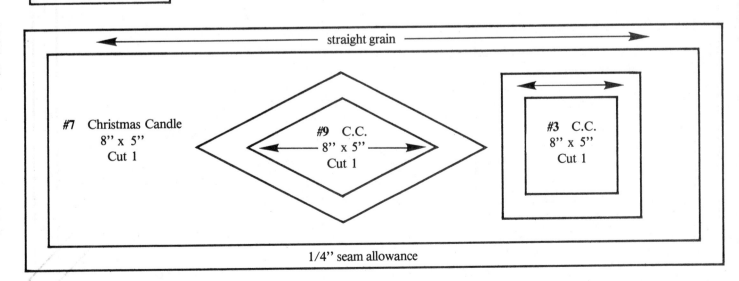

straight grain

#7 Christmas Candle
8" x 5"
Cut 1

#9 C.C.
8" x 5"
Cut 1

#3 C.C.
8" x 5"
Cut 1

1/4" seam allowance

DELECTABLE MOUNTAINS

Wall Quilt 30" x 30"

Delectable Mountains is an allover quilt design. It is particularly appealing as a Christmas wall quilt with a star in the middle. Lois Odell's version on page 34 features an intricate quilting motif in the center space. The many triangles in this design could easily be made with the Bias-Strip Piecing technique described on page 67.

Fabric Requirements

45"-wide, preshrunk & tested for color fastness
1/4 yd. red
1/2 yd. green (for piecing & binding)
1 yd. white
1 yd. backing
1 yd. batting
Thread, etc.

Piecing Sequence

#1   Delectable Mountains
Cut 1 red
+ 4 white

straight grain

#3   Delectable Mountains
Cut 4 green

1/4" seam allowance

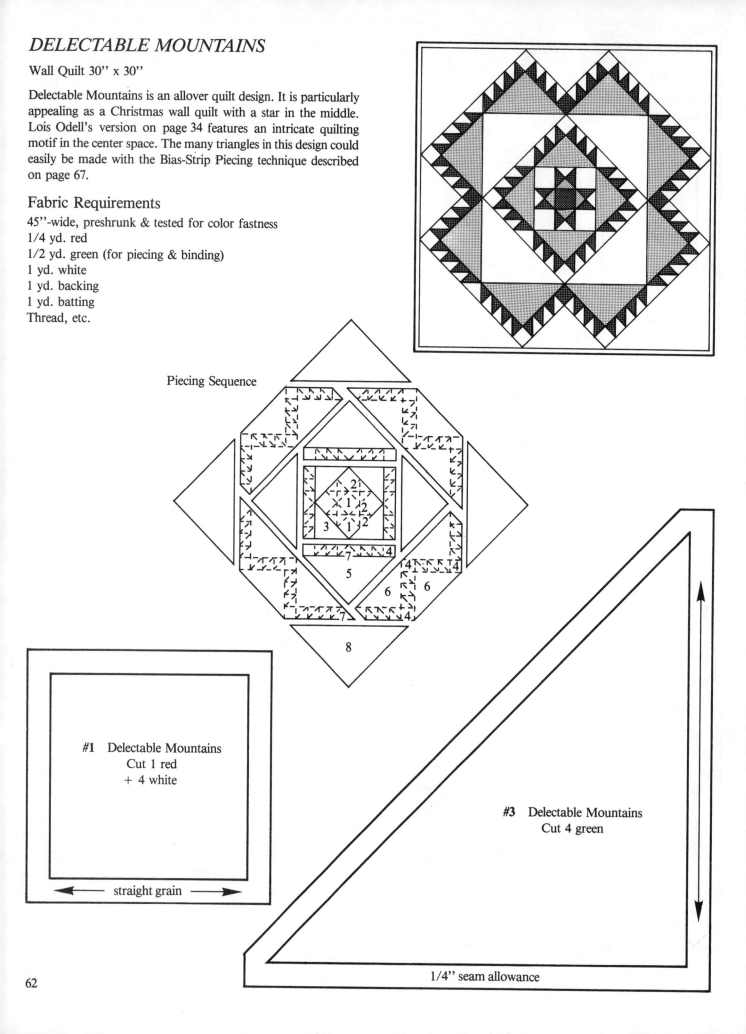

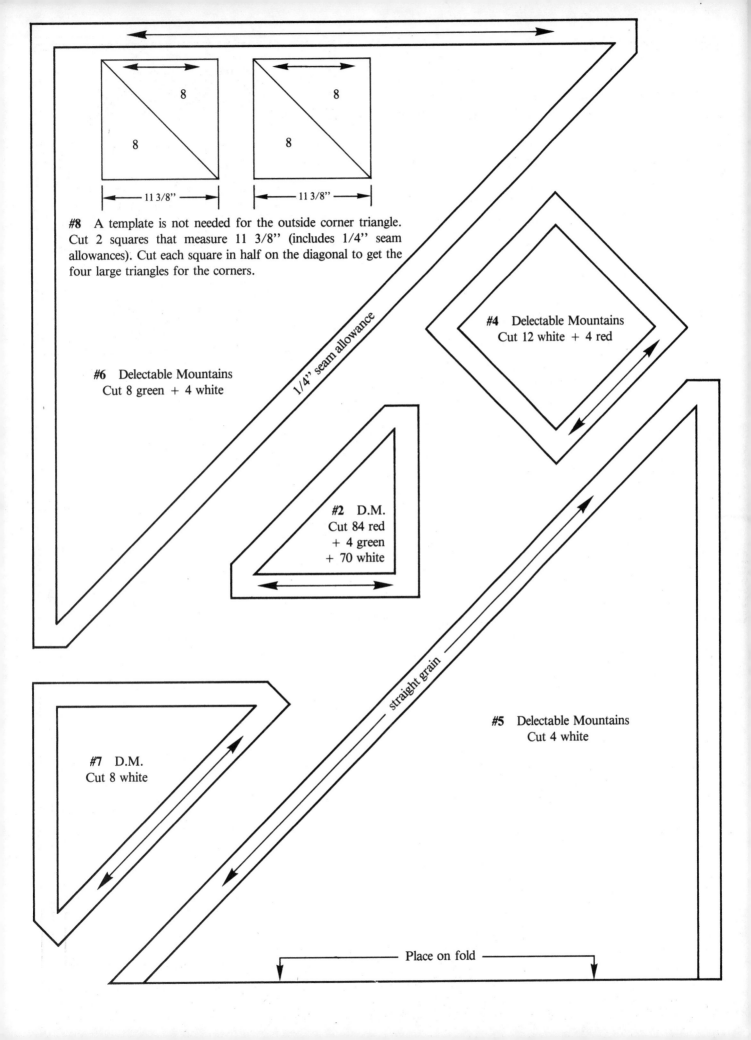

8

8

8

8

← 11 3/8" →   ← 11 3/8" →

#8 A template is not needed for the outside corner triangle. Cut 2 squares that measure 11 3/8" (includes 1/4" seam allowances). Cut each square in half on the diagonal to get the four large triangles for the corners.

1/4" seam allowance

#6 Delectable Mountains
Cut 8 green + 4 white

#4 Delectable Mountains
Cut 12 white + 4 red

#2 D.M.
Cut 84 red
+ 4 green
+ 70 white

straight grain

#7 D.M.
Cut 8 white

#5 Delectable Mountains
Cut 4 white

Place on fold

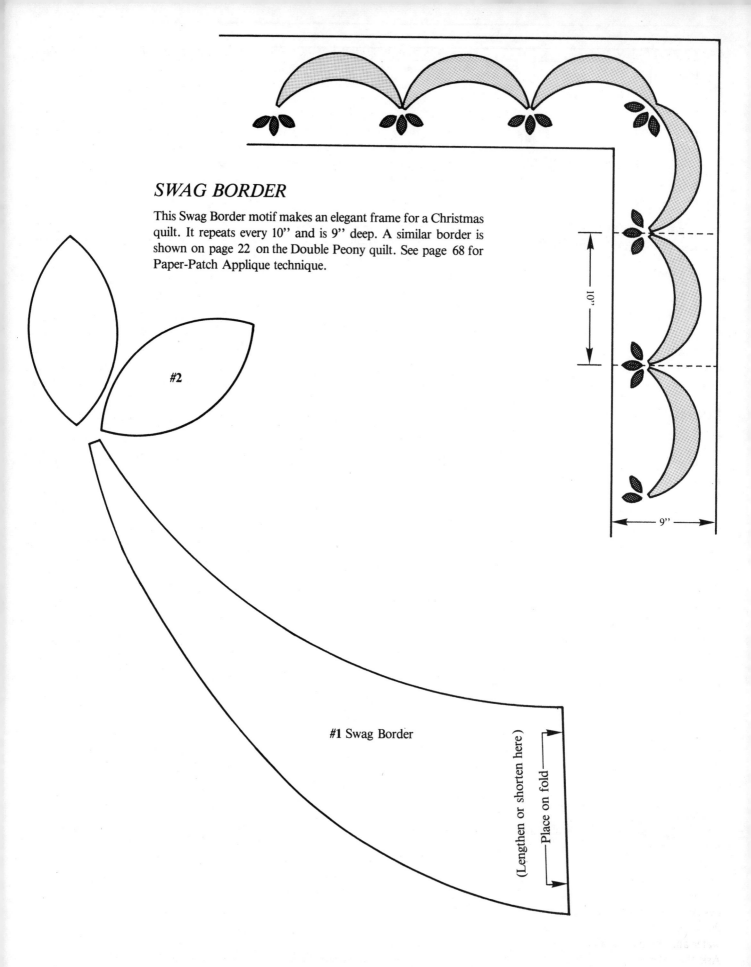

SWAG BORDER

This Swag Border motif makes an elegant frame for a Christmas quilt. It repeats every 10'' and is 9'' deep. A similar border is shown on page 22 on the Double Peony quilt. See page 68 for Paper-Patch Applique technique.

#2

10''

9''

#1 Swag Border

(Lengthen or shorten here)

Place on fold

GLOSSARY OF TECHNIQUES

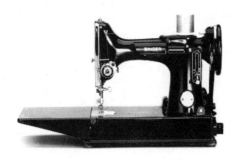

Tools and Supplies

Drawing Supplies: Graph paper in a 1/8" grid and colored pencils for drawing quilt plans and sketching design ideas.

Rulers: I use two rulers; both are clear plastic with a red grid of 1/8" squares. A short ruler is for drawing quilt designs on graph paper,; a longer one, 2" wide and 18" long, is for drafting designs full size, making templates, measuring and marking borders and quilting lines. If your local quilt shop doesn't carry them, try a stationery store or any place that carries drafting or art supplies. Another useful tool is a 12" plastic 45°/90° right angle.

Scissors: You will need scissors for paper, a good sharp pair for cutting fabric only, and possibly a little pair for snipping threads. If your fabric scissors are dull, have them sharpened. If they are close to "dead", invest in a new pair. It's worth it.

Template Material: To make templates, you will need graph paper or tracing paper, lightweight posterboard (manila file folders are good) or plastic, and a glue stick.

Markers: Most marking on fabric can be done with a regular #2 lead pencil and a white dressmaker's pencil. Keep them sharp. There is a blue felt tip marking pen available that is water erasable; it works especially well for marking quilting designs. (When you no longer need the lines for guides, spray them with cool water and the blue marks will disappear.) Ask the salespeople at a local fabric or quilt shop about the different kinds of marking pens available.

Sewing Machine: It needn't be fancy. All you need is an evenly locking straight stitch. Whatever kind of sewing machine you have, get to know it and how it runs. If it needs servicing, have it done, or get out the manual and do it yourself. Replace the old needle with a new one. Often, if your machine has a zigzag stitch, it will have a throat plate with an oblong hole for the needle to pass through. You might want to replace this plate with one that has a little round hole for straight stitching. This will help eliminate problems you might have with the edges of fabrics being fed into the hole by the action of the feed dogs.

Needles: A supply of new sewing machine needles for light to medium weight cottons is necessary. You'll also need an assortment of Sharps for handwork and quilting needles (Between #8, #9 or #10) if you plan to hand quilt.

Pins: Multi-colored glass or plastic-headed pins are generally longer, stronger and easier to see and hold than regular dressmaker's pins.

Iron and Ironing Board: A shot of steam is useful.

Seam Ripper: I always keep one handy.

Cutting

Study the design and templates. Determine the number of pieces to cut of each shape and each fabric. Trim the selvage from the fabric before you begin cutting. When one fabric is to be used both for borders and in the unit block designs, cut the borders first and the smaller pieces from what is left over (see Borders on page 43).

At the ironing board, press and fold the fabric so that one, two or four layers can be cut at one time (except for linear prints such as stripes and checks that should be cut one at a time). Fold the fabric so that each piece will be cut on the straight grain.

Position stiffened templates on the fabric so the arrows match the straight grain of the fabric. With a sharp pencil (white for dark fabrics, lead for light ones), trace around the template on the fabric. This is the cutting line. Cut just inside this line to most accurately duplicate the template.

In machine piecing, there are no drawn lines to guide your sewing. The seamline is 1/4" from the cut edge of the fabric, so this outside edge must be precisely cut to ensure accurate sewing.

Machine Piecing

For machine piecing, use white or neutral thread as light in color as the lightest fabric in the project. Use a dark neutral thread for piecing dark solids. It is easier to work with 100% cotton thread on some machines. Check your needle. If it is dull, burred or bent, replace it with a fresh one.

Sew exact 1/4" seams. To determine the 1/4" seam allowance on your machine, place a template under the presser foot and gently lower the needle onto the seamline. The distance from the needle to the edge of the template is 1/4". Lay a piece of masking tape at the edge of the template to act as the 1/4" mark; use the edge as a guide. Stitch length should be set at 10-12 stitches per inch. For most of the sewing in this book, sew from cut edge to cut edge (exceptions will be noted). Backtack, if you wish, although it is really not necessary as each seam will be crossed and held by another.

Use chain piecing whenever possible to save time and thread. To chain piece, sew one seam, but do not lift the presser foot. Do not take the piece out of the sewing machine and do not cut the thread. Instead, set up the next seam to be sewn and stitch as you did the first. There will be a little twist of thread between the two pieces. Sew all the seams you can at one time in this way, then remove the "chain". Clip the threads.

Press the seam allowances to one side, toward the darker fabric when possible. Avoid too much ironing as you sew because it tends to stretch biases and distort fabric shapes.

To piece a unit block, sew the smallest pieces together first to form units. Join smaller units to form larger ones until the block is complete.

Chain piecing

Short seams need not be pinned unless matching is involved, or the seam is longer than 4". Keep pins away from the seamline. Sewing over pins tends to burr the needle and makes it hard to be accurate in tight places.

Here are five matching techniques that can be helpful in many different piecing situations.

1. Opposing Seams: When stitching one seamed unit to another, press seam allowances on the seams that need to match in opposite directions. The two "opposing" seams will hold each other in place and evenly distribute the bulk. Plan pressing to take advantage of opposing seams.

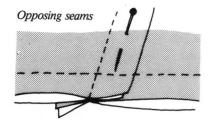

Opposing seams

2. Positioning Pin: A pin, carefully pushed straight through two points that need to match and pulled tight, will establish the proper point of matching. Pin the seam normally and remove the positioning pin before stitching.

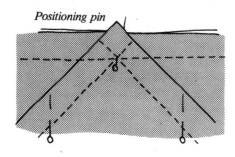

Positioning pin

66

3. The "X" : When triangles are pieced, stitches will form an "X" at the next seamline. Stitch through the center of the "X" to make sure the points on the sewn triangles will not be chopped off.

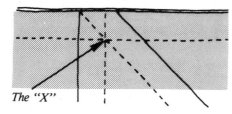

The "X"

4. Easing: When two pieces to be sewn together are supposed to match but instead are slightly different lengths, pin the points of matching and stitch with the shorter piece on top. The feed dogs ease the fullness of the bottom piece.

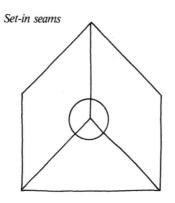

Set-in seams

5. Set-in seams: Where three seam lines come together at an angle, stop all stitching at the 1/4" seam line and backtack. Don't let even one stitch extend into the seam allowance. As each seam is finished, take the work out of the machine, position the next seam and start stitching in the new direction. Backtacking is necessary because these seamlines will not be crossed and held by any other stitches.

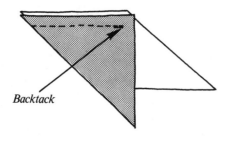

Backtack

Strip Piecing

Strip piecing is a method for sewing patchwork units together quickly by machine. Long fabric strips are sewn together in units called strata and then cut into shorter portions; the small units are then recombined to form simple designs. The technique is similar to Seminole piecing, but here the shapes are usually used in traditional patchwork instead of decorative bands for clothing and other projects.

Study the quilts in the gallery section and the unit block patterns for the feasibility of strip piecing. I would use strip techniques for the Double Ninepatch, Goose in the Pond, Bear's Paw, Georgetown Circle, Radiant Star, the tree patterns, striped lattices and sawtooth borders.

Straight-Grain Strip Piecing

Use straight-grain strip piecing when working with squares and rectangles. For instance, to make the triple lattice sections in the Feathered Star Sampler on page 20, three long strips (red, white, red) were sewn together, then cut to the proper length. Similarly, the ninepatch units in the Goose in the Pond quilt on page 39 were made by strip piecing, forming two sets of strips (red, green, red and green, red, green).

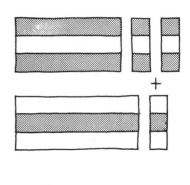

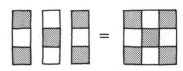

It is best to cut strips from the lengthwise grain of the fabric. When it is necessary to use the cross-grain to get the required length, be sure to straighten the fabric so strips will be cut exactly on-grain.

Press the fabric well before cutting strips. The accuracy of the piecing will depend largely on how carefully fabric, strips and seams are pressed.

To determine the width to cut strips, add a 1/4" seam allowance to each side of the finished strip. For example, if the finished dimension of the piece will be 1", cut 1 1/2" strips. Stack the fabric before marking and cutting so two or four layers can be cut at one time. Mark strips and cut with sharp scissors or a rotary cutter. Try to be accurate; speed piecing does not mean sloppy piecing.

Sew long strips together with 1/4" seam allowances, but wait to press until all the strips in the unit have been sewn. Press seam allowances toward the darker fabric, and press from the right side of the work so the fabric won't pleat along the seamlines. Use templates or simply measure distances to mark locations for crosswise cuts.

Bias-Strip Piecing

Use bias-strip piecing when working with triangles. Half-square triangles and quarter-square triangles, as well as many other shapes, can be cut using this method. It is extremely accurate and especially useful for very small half-square units like the "feathers" on a Feathered Star.

Half-square triangles

Quarter-square triangles

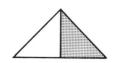

Making bias strips

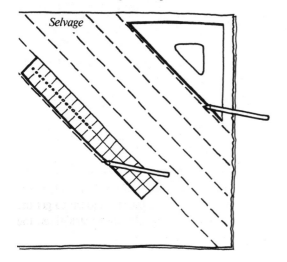

Selvage

Begin by cutting two strips of bias grain fabric, one dark and one light.

Layer the two fabrics, mark the top layer as shown, and cut two strips at a time. To determine the width of the bias strips, measure the square template to be used from corner to corner (including seam allowances) on the diagonal. Add 3" and divide by 2.

$$\frac{X'' + 3''}{2} = \text{width of each bias strip}$$

Sew the strips together on the long bias edge, using 1/4" seam allowance. Press seams open or toward the dark fabric. Place a stiffened square template on the right side of the bias strip unit with opposite corners lined up with the seamline. Trace around the template. Start at one end and make a string of squares the length of the seamline. Carefully cut out the fabric squares, cutting only on the drawn lines (actually right inside the drawn lines). This will yield several squares made of two triangles with outside edges on the straight grain of the fabric. There will be two funny shaped pieces left over. Seam the long straight edges of these together, press, and make another set of squares.

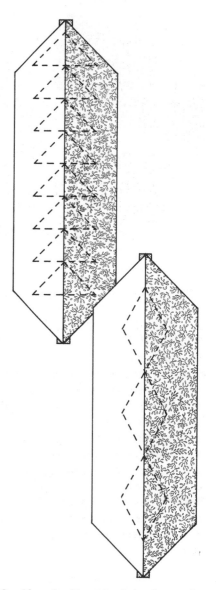

Consider using bias-strip piecing for any shape consisting of two equal triangles.

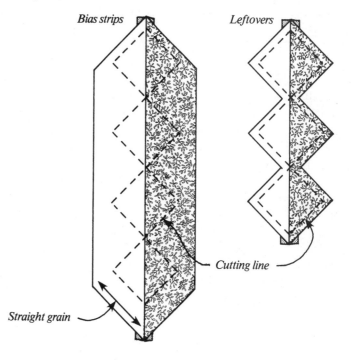

Bias strips

Leftovers

Cutting line

Straight grain

Paper-Patch Applique

1. Make a stiffened template of each shape in the applique design. Do not add seam allowances to the templates.

2. On bond weight paper, trace around the stiffened templates to make a paper patch for each shape in the applique.

3. Pin each paper patch to the wrong side of the fabric.

4. Cut out fabric shapes, adding 1/4" seam allowance around each paper shape.

5. With your fingers, turn the seam allowance over the edge of the paper and baste to paper. Baste inside curves first (a little clipping may be necessary to help the fabric stretch). On outside curves, take small running stitches through fabric only to ease in fullness. Take an occasional stitch through the paper to hold fabric in place. This basting order (inside curves first, outside curves last) is also followed when appliqueing fabric to the block and allows fullness and bias stretch to be eased outward.

6. When all the seam allowances are turned and basted, press the applique pieces. Then position and pin the pieces in place on the background material.

7. Using a small, blind hemming stitch and a single matching thread (i.e., green thread for a green leaf), applique shapes to the background.

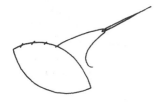

8. Before the stitching on each piece is completed, the paper patch must be removed. To take the paper out, leave a small opening unstitched. Remove all the basting threads. Pull the paper out through the opening and finish stitching.

Mitering Corners

1. Prepare the borders. Determine the finished outside dimensions of your quilt. Cut the borders this length plus 1/2" for seam allowances. When using a striped fabric for the borders, make sure the design on all four borders is cut the same way. Multiple borders should be sewn together and the resulting "striped" units treated as a single border for mitering.

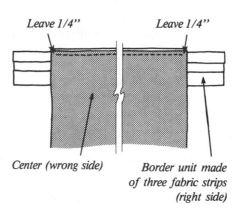

Center (wrong side)

Border unit made of three fabric strips (right side)

2. To attach the border to the pieced section of the quilt, center each border on a side so the ends extend equally on either side of the center section. Using a 1/4" seam allowance, sew the border to the center leaving 1/4" unsewn at the beginning and end of the stitching line. Press the seam allowances toward the border.

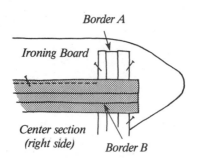

Border A

Ironing Board

Center section (right side)

Border B

3. Arrange the first corner to be mitered on the ironing board as illustrated. Press the corner flat and straight. To prevent it from slipping, pin the quilt to the ironing board. Following the illustration, turn border "B" right side up, folding the corner to be mitered under at a 45° angle. Match the raw edges underneath with those of border "A". Fuss with it until it looks good. The stripes and border designs should meet. Check the squareness of the corner with a right angle. Press the fold. This will be the sewing line. Pin the borders together to prevent shifting and unpin the piece from the board. Turn wrong side out and pin along the fold line, readjusting if necessary to match the designs.

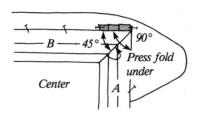

B — 45°   90°
Press fold under
Center   A

4. Machine baste from the inside to the outside corner on the fold line, leaving 1/4" at the beginning unsewn. Check for accuracy. If it is right, sew again with a regular stitch. Backtack at the beginning and end of the stitching line. (After you have mitered several times, the basting step ceases to be necessary.) Trim the excess fabric 1/4" along the mitered seam. Press this seam open. Press the other seams to the outside.

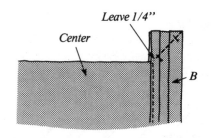

Leave 1/4"
Center
B

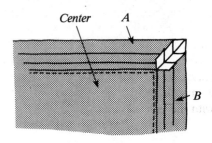

Center   A
B

Preparing to Quilt

Marking

In most cases, before you quilt, the quilt top must be marked with lines to guide stitching. Where you place the quilting lines will depend on the patchwork design, the type of batting used, and how much quilting you want to do. You can mark an allover, straight-line pattern, such as a grid of squares or parallel diagonal lines. Or, you can outline quilt the design either "in the ditch" (close to but not on the seamlines) or 1/4" away on each side of every seamline, for which no marking is required. There are many pretty, traditional quilting motifs that fit nicely in plain areas, such as unpieced blocks and borders. Try to avoid quilting too close to the seamlines, where the bulk of seam allowances might slow you down or make the stitches uneven. Keep in mind also that the purpose of quilting, besides its esthetic value, is to securely hold the three layers together. Don't leave large areas unquilted.

Thoroughly press the quilt top and mark it before it is assembled with the batting and backing. You will need marking pencils, a long ruler or yardstick, stencils or templates for quilting motifs, and a smooth, clean hard surface on which to work. Use a sharp marking pencil and lightly mark the quilting lines on the fabric. No matter what kind of marking tool is used, light lines will be easier to remove than heavy ones.

Backing

A single length of 45"-wide fabric can often be used for backing small quilts. To be safe, plan on a useable width of only 42" after shrinkage and cutting off selvages. For larger quilts, two lengths of fabric will have to be sewn together to get one large enough.

Cut the backing an inch larger than the quilt top all the way around. Press thoroughly with seams open. Lay the backing face down on a large, clean, flat surface. With masking tape, tape the backing down (without stretching) to keep it smooth and flat while you are working with the other layers.

Batting

Batting is the filler in a quilt or comforter. Thick batting is used in comforters that are tied. If you plan to quilt, use thin batting and quilt by hand.

Thin batting comes in 100% polyester, 100% cotton and a cotton-polyester (80%-20%) combination. All cotton batting requires close quilting to prevent shifting and separating in the wash. Most old quilts have cotton batting and are rather flat. Cotton is a good natural fiber that lasts well and is compatible with cotton and cotton-blend fabrics. Less quilting is required on 100% polyester batting. If polyester batting is glazed or bonded, it is easy to work with, won't pull apart and has more loft than cotton. Some polyester batting, however, has a tendency to "beard". This "fiber migration" (the small white polyester fibers creep to the quilt's surface between the threads in the fabric) happens mostly when polyester blends are used instead of 100% cotton fabrics. The cotton-polyester combination batting is supposed to combine the best features of the two fibers. A single layer of preshrunk cotton flannel can be used for filler instead of batting. The quilt will be very flat, and the quilting stitches highly visible.

Cut the batting the same size as the quilt backing and lay it gently on top.

Assembling the Layers

Center the freshly ironed and marked quilt top on top of the batting, face up. Starting in the middle, pin baste the three layers together while gently smoothing out fullness to the sides and corners. Take care not to distort the straight lines of the quilt design and the borders.

After pinning, baste the layers together with needle and light colored thread. Start in the middle and make a line of large stitches to each corner to form a large X. Continue basting in a grid of parallel lines 6" to 8" apart. Finish with a row of basting around the outside edges. Quilts to be quilted with a hoop or on your lap will be handled more than those quilted on a frame; therefore, they will require more basting.

After basting, remove the pins. Now you are ready to quilt.

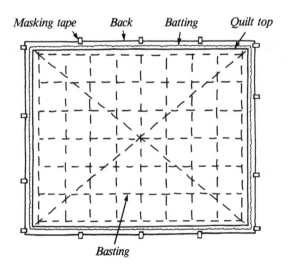

Masking tape   Back   Batting   Quilt top

Basting

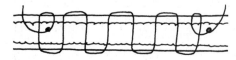
Hand quilting stitch

Hand Quilting

To quilt by hand, you will need quilting thread, quilting needles, small scissors, a thimble and perhaps a balloon or large rubber band to help grasp the needle if it gets stuck. Quilt on a frame, a large hoop, or just on your lap or a table. Use a single strand of quilting thread no longer than 18''. Make a small single knot in the end of the thread. The quilting stitch is a small running stitch that goes through all three layers of the quilt. Take two, three or even four stitches at a time if you can keep them even. When crossing seams, you might find it necessary to "hunt and peck" one stitch at a time.

To begin, insert the needle in the top layer about 3/4'' from the point you want to start stitching. Pull the needle out at the starting point and gently tug at the knot until it pops through the fabric and is buried in the batting. Make a backstitch and begin quilting. Stitches should be tiny (8 to 10 per inch is good), even and straight. At first, concentrate on even and straight; tiny will come with practice.

When you come almost to the end of the thread, make a single knot fairly close to the fabric. Make a backstitch to bury the knot in the batting. Run the thread off through the batting and out the quilt top. Snip it off. The first and last stitches look different from the running stitches between. To make them less noticeable, start and stop where quilting lines cross each other or at seam joints.

Binding

After quilting, trim excess batting and backing to the edge of the quilt front. Finish the raw edges with bias binding. Bias binding can be purchased by the package or by the yard, or you can make your own.

To make bias binding from yardage, press a single layer of fabric. Use a 12'' right angle to establish the bias (45° angle) of the fabric by aligning one of the angle's short sides with the selvage. Draw a line on the fabric along the 45° angle. Using this first marked line as a guide, draw several more parallel lines, each 2'' apart. You'll find the 2''-wide plastic ruler very handy for this procedure. Cut the strips and seam them together where necessary to get a bias strip long enough for each side of the quilt (the length of the side plus 2'').

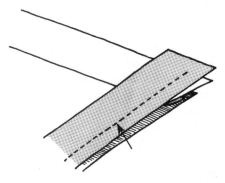
Overlapping bias binding at quilt corners

Using the "even-feed" presser foot and a 1/2'' seam allowance, sew the binding strips to the front of the quilt. Be careful not to stretch the bias or the quilt edge as you sew. If your machine doesn't have an "even-feed" foot, sometimes it is best to put the binding on entirely by hand. Overlap the corners. Fold under the raw edge of the binding on the back side of the quilt. Pin it in place. Enclose the raw edges at the corners. Using thread to match the binding, hand sew the binding in place with a hemming stitch.

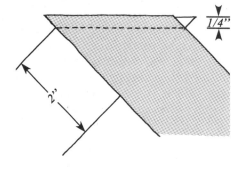

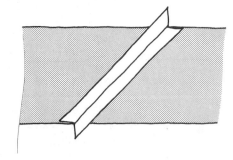

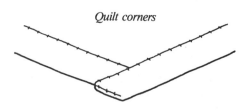
Quilt corners

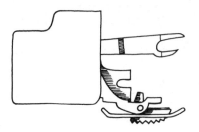

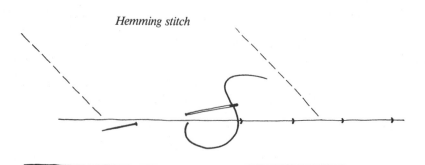
Hemming stitch

BIBLIOGRAPHY

Barnett, James H., THE AMERICAN CHRISTMAS, The MacMillan Company, New York, 1954.

Beyer, Jinny, THE QUILTER'S ALBUM OF BLOCKS AND BORDERS, McLean, Virginia: EPM Publiations, Inc., 1980.

Brackman, Barbara, "Old Time Quilting, Poinsettias", Quilter's Newsletter Magazine, Nov/Dec 1980, p. 20.

Brackman, Barbara, "Dating Old Quilts, Part One: Green Prints and Dyes", Quilter's Newsletter Magazine, Sept. 1984, p. 24.

Brackman, Barbara, "Dating Old Quilts, Part Six: Style and Pattern as Clues", Quilter's Newsletter Magazine, March 1985, p. 22.

Bradkin, Cheryl Greider, THE SEMINOLE PATCHWORK BOOK, Atlanta, Georgia: Yours Truly, 1980.

Del Re, Gerard and Patricia, THE CHRISTMAS ALMANACK, Garden City, New York: Doubleday & Company, Inc., 1979.

Finley, Ruth E., OLD PATCHWORK QUILTS, Charles T. Branford Company, 1983.

Foley, Daniel J., THE CHRISTMAS TREE, Philadelphia, Pennsylvania: Chilton Company, 1960.

Hall, Carrie A. and Rose G. Krestinger, THE ROMANCE OF THE PATCHWORK QUILT, New York, New York: Bonanza Books, 1935.

Holstein, Jonathan, THE PIECED QUILT, AN AMERICAN DESIGN TRADITION, Greenwich, Connecticut: New York Graphic Society Ltd., 1973.

Irwin, John Rice, A PEOPLE AND THEIR QUILTS, Exton, Pennsylvania: Schiffer Publishing Limited, 1983.

Johannah, Barbara, THE QUICK QUILTMAKING HANDBOOK, Menlo Park, California: Pride of the Forest, 1979.

Martin, Judy, THE PATCHWORKBOOK, New York, New York: Charles Scribner's Sons, 1983.

McCloskey, Marsha R., SMALL QUILTS, Bothell, Washington: That Patchwork Place, Inc., 1982.

McCloskey, Marsha R., WALL QUILTS, Bothell, Washington: That Patchwork Place, Inc., 1983.

McCloskey, Marsha R., PROJECTS FOR BLOCKS AND BORDERS, Bothell, Washington: That Patchwork Place, Inc., 1984.

McKelvey, Susan Richardson, COLOR FOR QUILTERS, Atlanta, Georgia: Yours Truly, 1984.

McKim, Ruby, 101 PATCHWORK PATTERNS, New York: Dover Publications, Inc., 1962.

Nelson, Cyril I. and Carter Houck, THE QUILT ENGAGEMENT CALENDAR TREASURY, New York, E.P. Dutton, Inc., 1982.

Nelson, Cyril I., THE QUILT ENGAGEMENT CALENDAR, New York, E.P. Dutton, Inc., 1982.

Nelson, Cyril I., THE QUILT ENGAGEMENT CALENDAR, New York, E.P. Dutton, Inc., 1985.

Orlofsky, Patsy and Myron, QUILTS IN AMERICA, New York, New York: McGraw Hill Book Co., 1974.

Safford, Carleton L. and Robert Bishop, AMERICA'S QUILTS AND COVERLETS, New York, New York: Weathervane Books, 1974.

Saltkill, Sue, COUNTRY CHRISTMAS, Bothell, Washington: That Patchwork Place, Inc., 1983.

Snyder, Phillip V., THE CHRISTMAS TREE BOOK, Middlesex, England: Penguin Books, 1983.

Webster, Marie D., QUILTS: THEIR STORY AND HOW TO MAKE THEM, Garden City, New York: Doubleday & Company, 1916.

PATTERN SOURCES

CHRISTMAS QUILT pattern (p. 13). Directions for crib, twin and double sized quilts. Quilter's Heaven, 21056 N.E. 117th St., Redmond, WA 98052. $6.00 ppd.

Quilter's Newsletter Magazine, Quilts and Other Comforts Catalogue, Box 394, 6700 W. 44th Ave., Wheatridge, CO 80033. CHRISTMAS MEMORY PATTERNS available from past Christmases beginning with 1970. Each pattern is $1.00; any two, $1.50, any four, $2.50; all thirteen in envelope are $6.00 ppd.

Stearns and Foster Catalogue. Creative Quilting Center, The Stearns and Foster Co., Lockland, Cincinnati, Ohio 45215. The POINSETTIA applique quilt pattern (p. 28) is #39 and GREAT GRANDMOTHER'S QUILT (p. 28) is #122. $2.00 ppd.

THAT PATCHWORK PLACE PUBLICATIONS

That Patchwork Place, Inc. P.O. Box 118, Bothell, WA 98041:

FEATHERED STAR SAMPLER (p. 20) by Marsha McCloskey.
Pattern $3.95.
COUNTRY CHRISTMAS by Sue Saltkill $6.00
A QUILTER'S CHRISTMAS by Nancyann Twelker $8.00
CHRISTMAS CLASSICS by Sue Saltkill $6.95

Christmas Cards and Note Cards available featuring Princess Feather, Feathered Star, Bed of Peonies and Rose Wreath quilts.

Forthcoming Publications:
CHRISTMAS CROSS STITCH by Suzanne Wall $5.95
TREE QUILTS by Carolann Palmer $9.95

Marsha McCloskey lives with her family in Seattle and teaches for quilting stores and special interest groups. She is the author of three books: SMALL QUILTS, WALL QUILTS, and PROJECTS FOR BLOCKS AND BORDERS, published by That Patchwork Place.

Printed in the United States of America